9/9/10

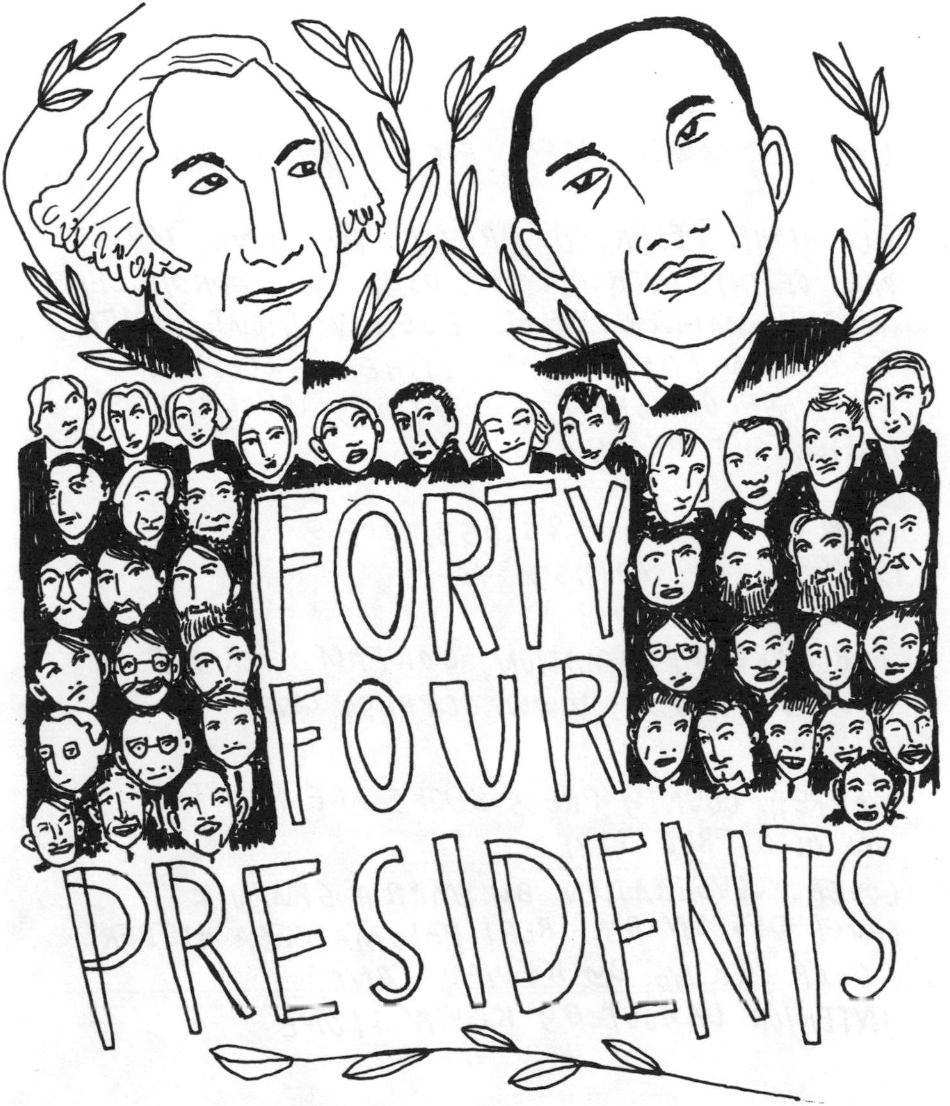
FORTY
FOUR
PRESIDENTS

GARRETT COUNTY PRESS FIRST EDITION 2009

ISBN-13: 978-1-891053-10-8
ISBN-10: 1-891053-10-8

FOR MORE INFORMATION, CONTACT GARRETT COUNTY PRESS: WWW. GCPRESS. COM

GARRETT COUNTY PRESS BOOKS ARE PRINTED ON ACID FREE PAPER.
COVER ILLUSTRATION BY MARIA SPUTNIK
COVER DESIGN BY IRERI PALOMA VEGA RIEDER
COVER INKING BY KEVIN STONE
INTERIOR LAYOUT BY KEVIN STONE

FORTY FOUR PRESIDENTS

1. GEORGE WASHINGTON

(1789-97, NO PARTY)

IS THE FIRST WHITE PRESIDENT.

2. JOHN ADAMS (1797-1801, FEDERALIST)

IS THE FIRST PRESIDENT NEVER TO OWN SLAVES IN HIS LIFETIME. HE IS ALSO THE FIRST OF FOUR PRESIDENTS NAMED JOHN.

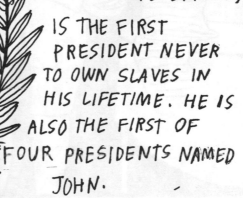

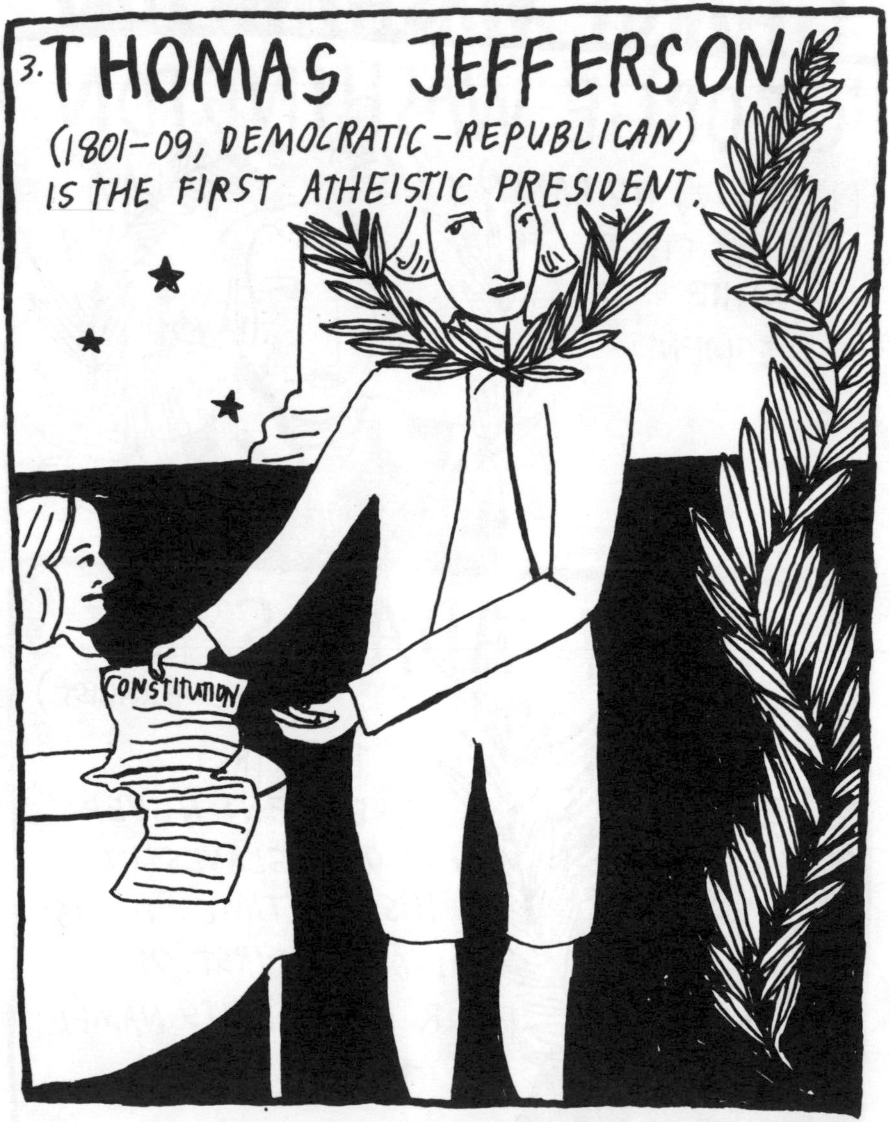
3. THOMAS JEFFERSON
(1801–09, DEMOCRATIC-REPUBLICAN)
IS THE FIRST ATHEISTIC PRESIDENT.
CONSTITUTION

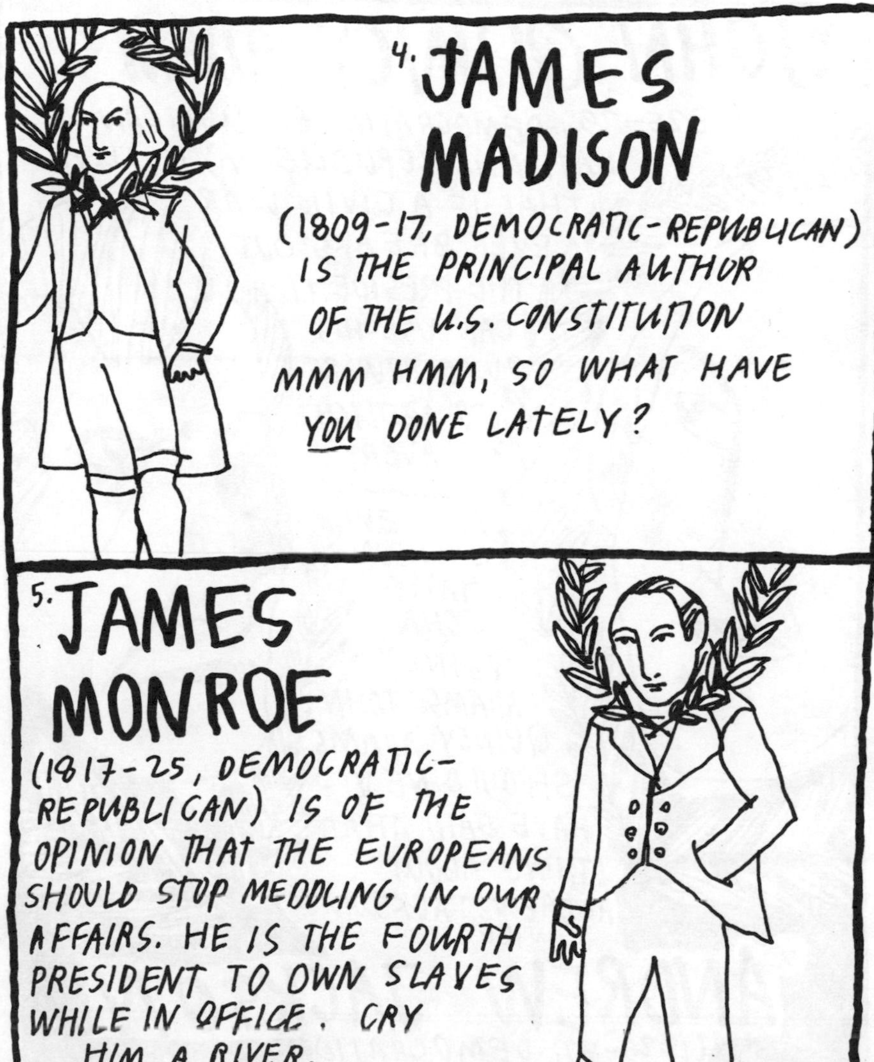
4. JAMES MADISON
(1809-17, DEMOCRATIC-REPUBLICAN) IS THE PRINCIPAL AUTHOR OF THE U.S. CONSTITUTION
MMM HMM, SO WHAT HAVE YOU DONE LATELY?
5. JAMES MONROE
(1817-25, DEMOCRATIC-REPUBLICAN) IS OF THE OPINION THAT THE EUROPEANS SHOULD STOP MEDDLING IN OUR AFFAIRS. HE IS THE FOURTH PRESIDENT TO OWN SLAVES WHILE IN OFFICE. CRY HIM A RIVER.

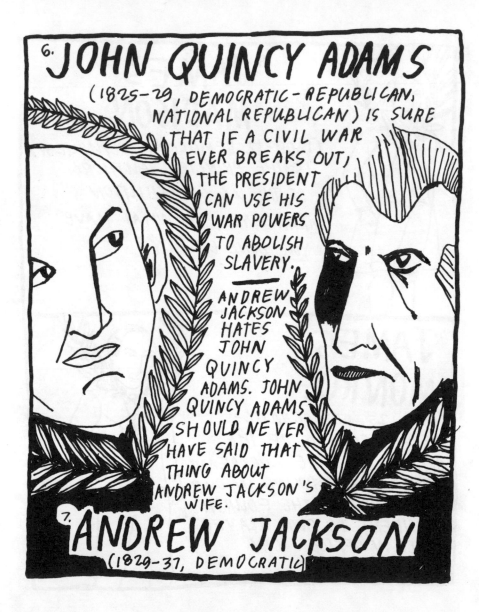

6. JOHN QUINCY ADAMS (1825-29, DEMOCRATIC-REPUBLICAN, NATIONAL REPUBLICAN) IS SURE THAT IF A CIVIL WAR EVER BREAKS OUT, THE PRESIDENT CAN USE HIS WAR POWERS TO ABOLISH SLAVERY.

ANDREW JACKSON HATES JOHN QUINCY ADAMS. JOHN QUINCY ADAMS SHOULD NEVER HAVE SAID THAT THING ABOUT ANDREW JACKSON'S WIFE.

7. ANDREW JACKSON (1829-37, DEMOCRATIC)

8. MARTIN VAN BUREN

(1837 – 41, DEMOCRATIC) IS THE FIRST PRESIDENT TO HAVE LEARNED ENGLISH AS A SECOND LANGUAGE.

9. WILLIAM HENRY HARRISON

(1841, WHIG)

IS THE FIRST PRESIDENT TO DIE IN OFFICE, WHICH EXPLAINS WHY HE ISN'T GOING TO FRIEND YOU BACK. on monday

BASIC INFORMATION
married to Anna Symmes
network: Indiana Territory

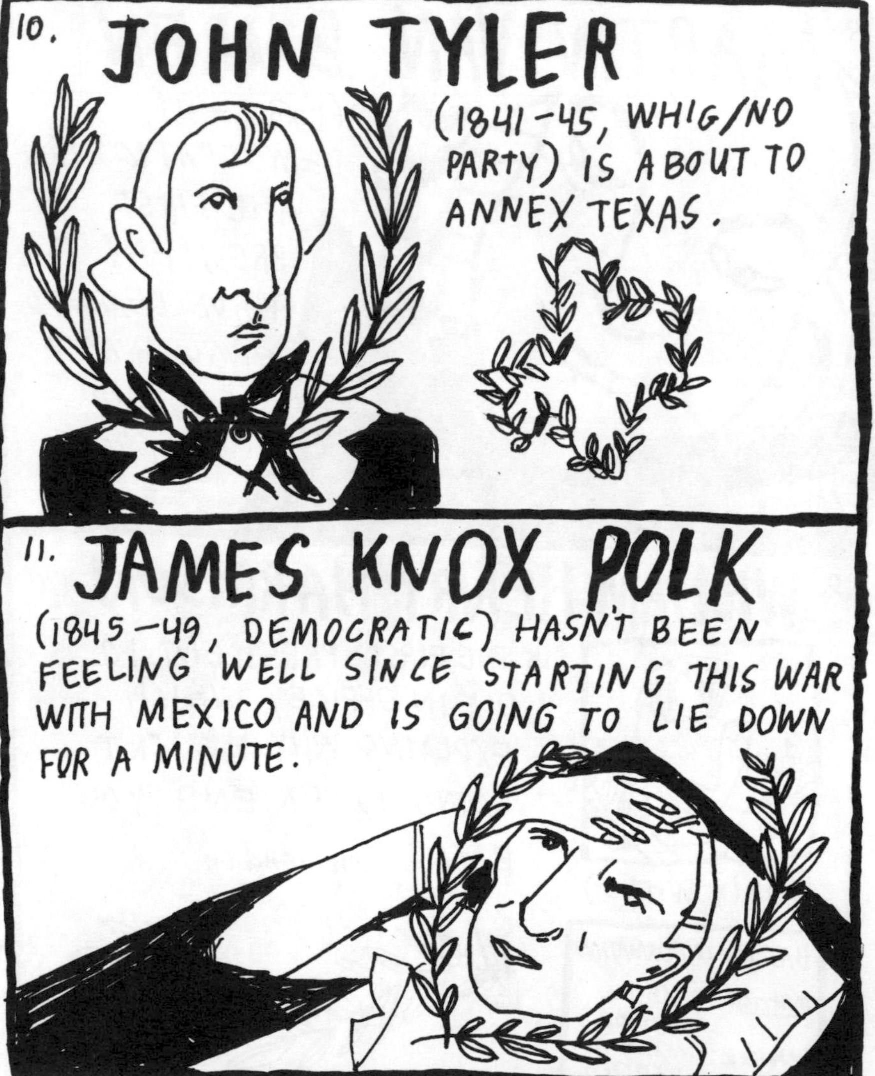

10. JOHN TYLER
(1841–45, WHIG/NO PARTY) IS ABOUT TO ANNEX TEXAS.
11. JAMES KNOX POLK
(1845–49, DEMOCRATIC) HASN'T BEEN FEELING WELL SINCE STARTING THIS WAR WITH MEXICO AND IS GOING TO LIE DOWN FOR A MINUTE.

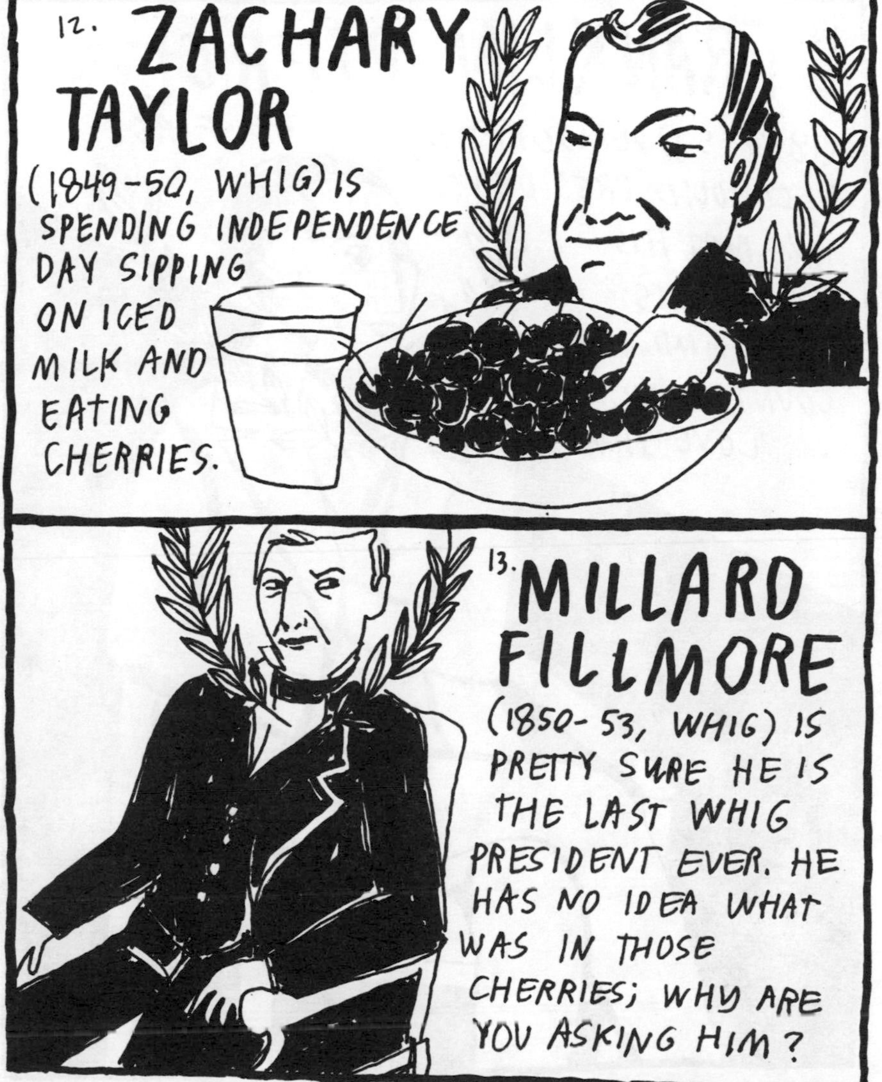
12. ZACHARY TAYLOR
(1849-50, WHIG) IS SPENDING INDEPENDENCE DAY SIPPING ON ICED MILK AND EATING CHERRIES.
13. MILLARD FILLMORE
(1850-53, WHIG) IS PRETTY SURE HE IS THE LAST WHIG PRESIDENT EVER. HE HAS NO IDEA WHAT WAS IN THOSE CHERRIES; WHY ARE YOU ASKING HIM?

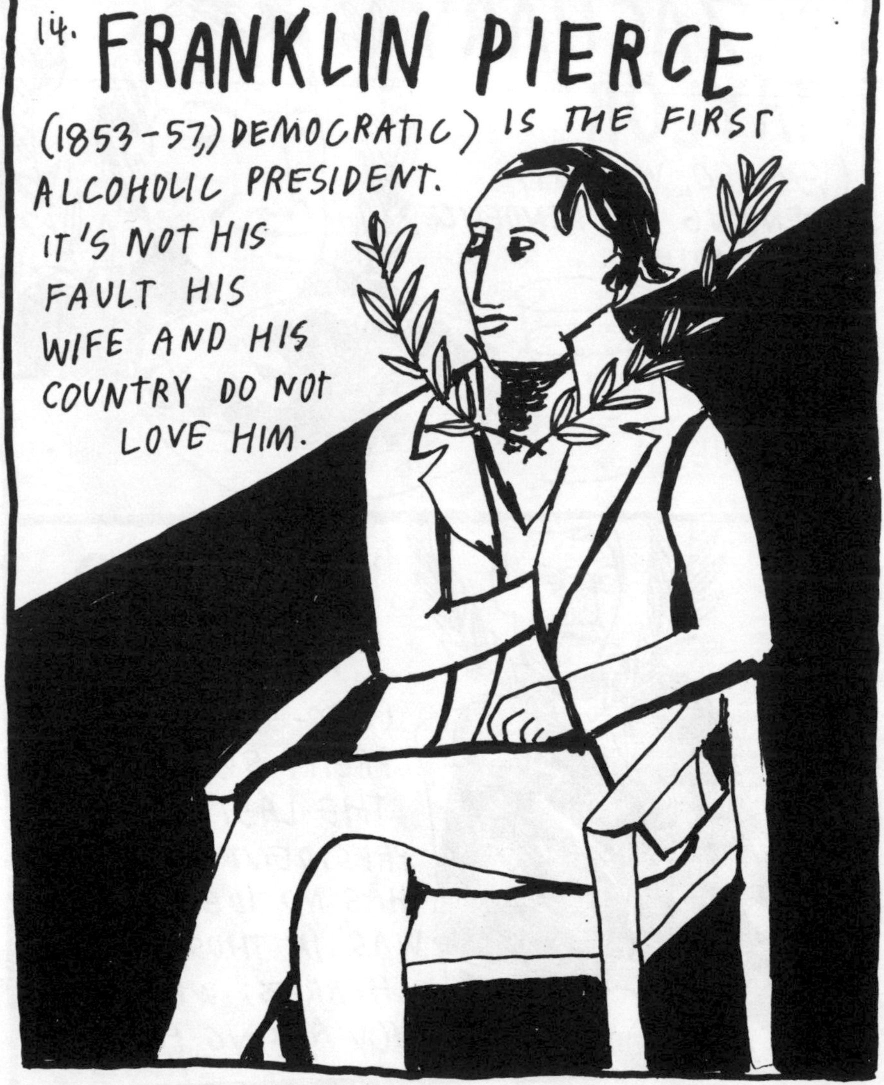
14. FRANKLIN PIERCE
(1853-57,) DEMOCRATIC) IS THE FIRST ALCOHOLIC PRESIDENT.
IT'S NOT HIS FAULT HIS WIFE AND HIS COUNTRY DO NOT LOVE HIM.

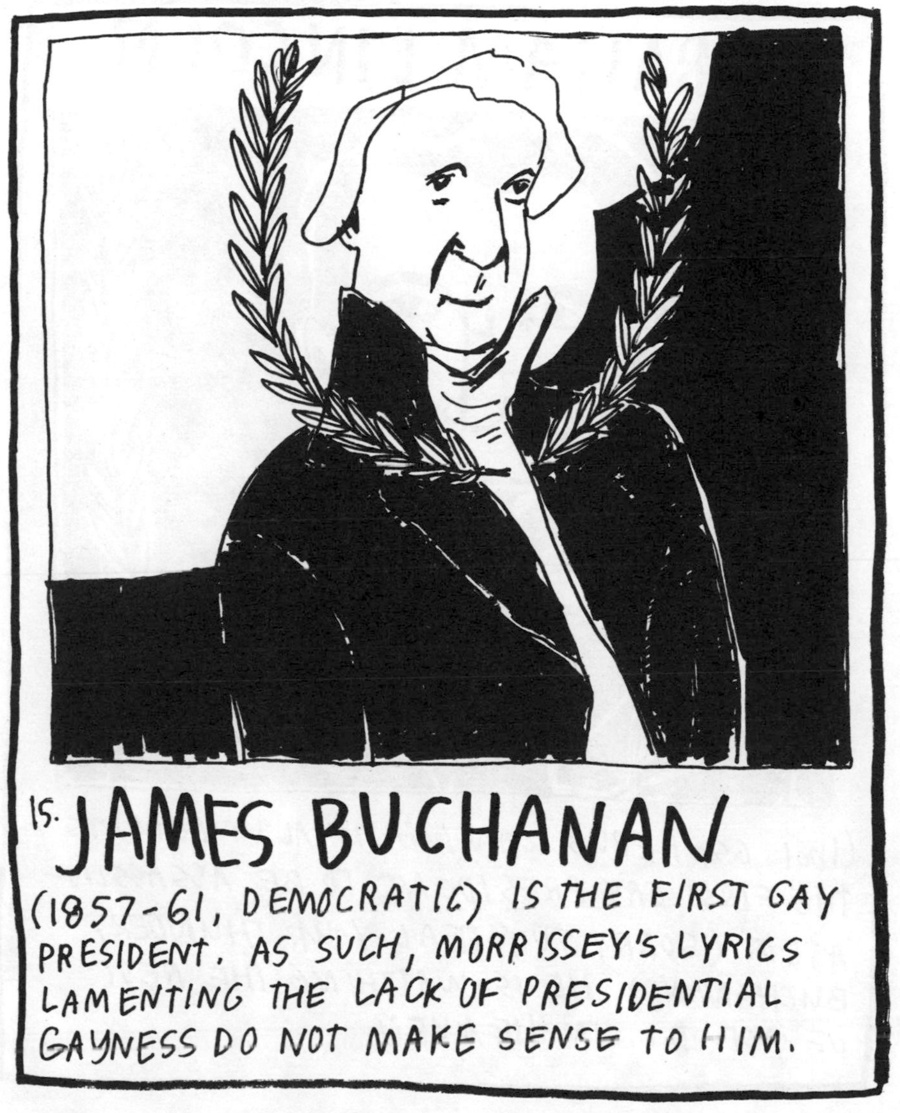

15. JAMES BUCHANAN

(1857-61, DEMOCRATIC) IS THE FIRST GAY PRESIDENT. AS SUCH, MORRISSEY'S LYRICS LAMENTING THE LACK OF PRESIDENTIAL GAYNESS DO NOT MAKE SENSE TO HIM.

16. ABRAHAM LINCOLN

(1861-65, REPUBLICAN / NATIONAL UNION) IS THE FIRST GAY PRESIDENT TO BE ASSASSINATED. (SORRY TO STEAL YOUR THUNDER, BUCHANAN.) HE IS WATCHING THE REST OF ACT III ... IN HEAVEN.

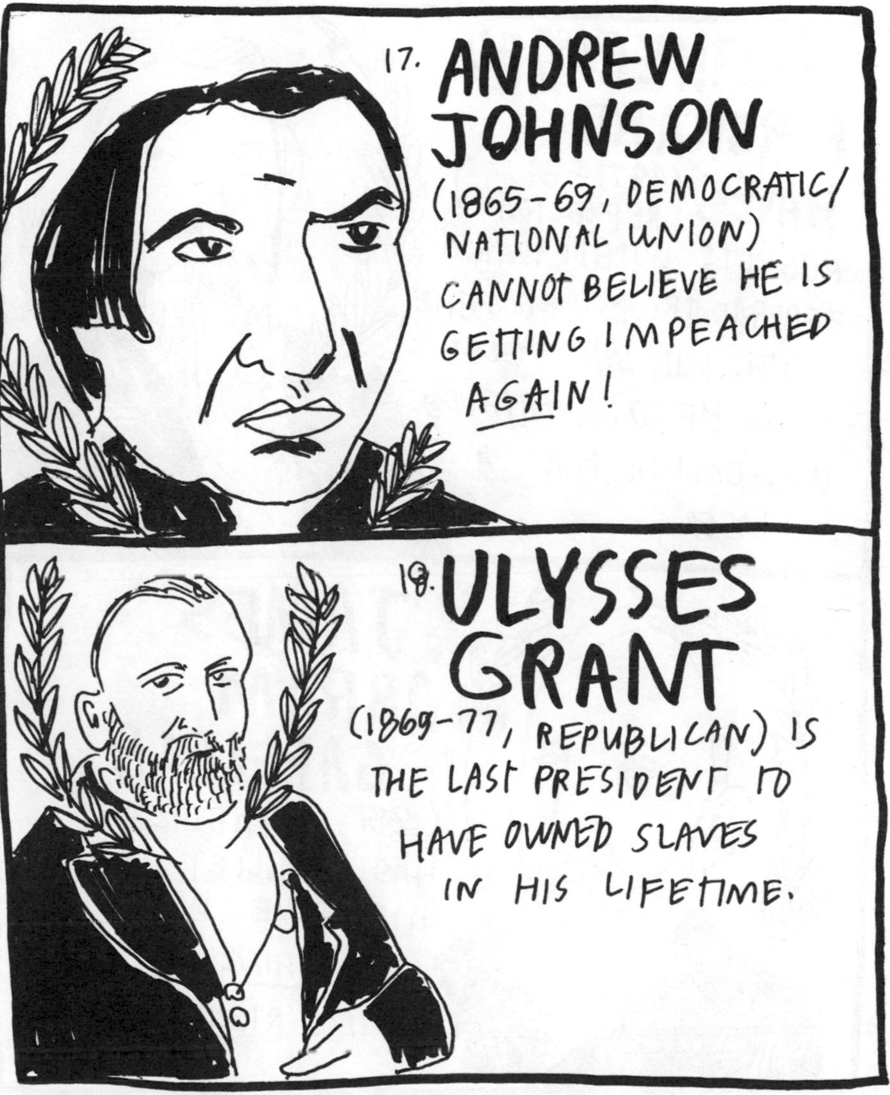
17. ANDREW JOHNSON
(1865-69, DEMOCRATIC/ NATIONAL UNION) CANNOT BELIEVE HE IS GETTING IMPEACHED AGAIN!
18. ULYSSES GRANT
(1869-77, REPUBLICAN) IS THE LAST PRESIDENT TO HAVE OWNED SLAVES IN HIS LIFETIME.

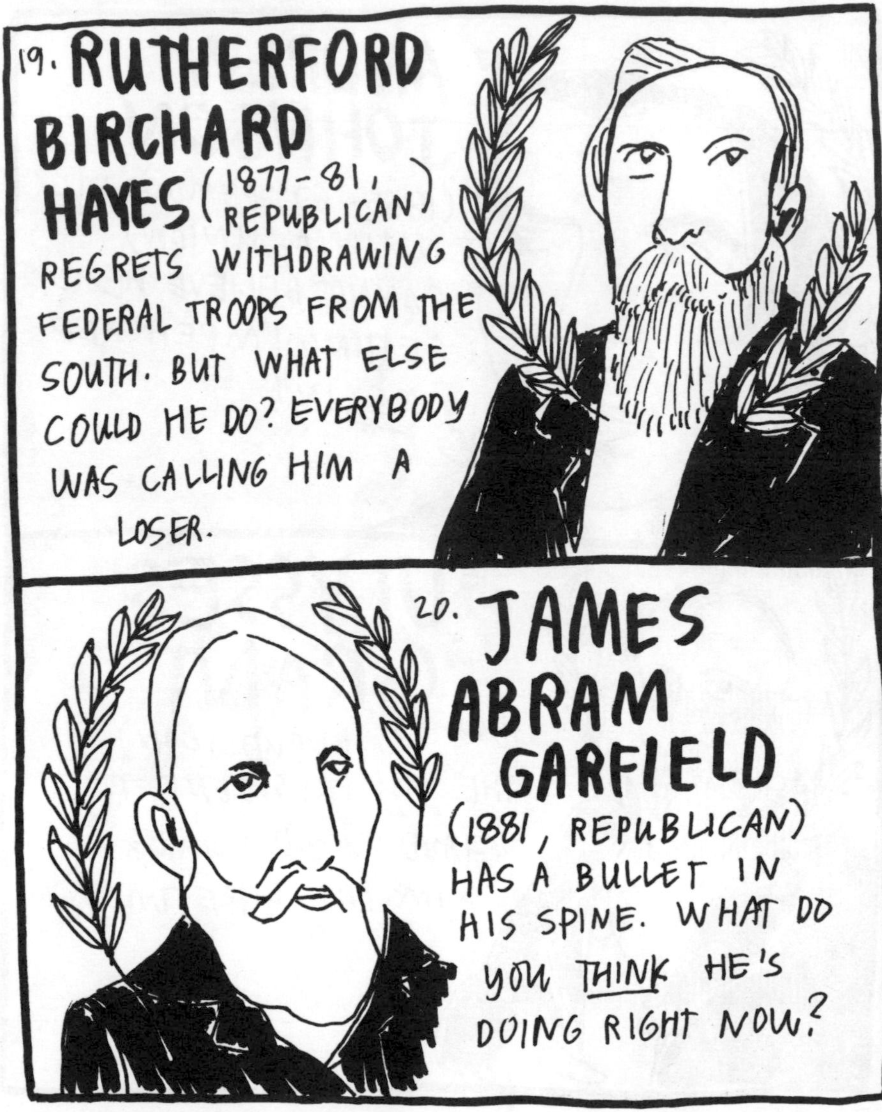
19. RUTHERFORD BIRCHARD HAYES (1877-81, REPUBLICAN)
REGRETS WITHDRAWING FEDERAL TROOPS FROM THE SOUTH. BUT WHAT ELSE COULD HE DO? EVERYBODY WAS CALLING HIM A LOSER.
20. JAMES ABRAM GARFIELD
(1881, REPUBLICAN)
HAS A BULLET IN HIS SPINE. WHAT DO YOU THINK HE'S DOING RIGHT NOW?

21. CHESTER ALAN ARTHUR

(1881–85), REPUBLICAN) IS LIKED BY MARK TWAIN, AND SOME DAYS THIS IS ENOUGH TO TAKE THE PAIN AWAY.

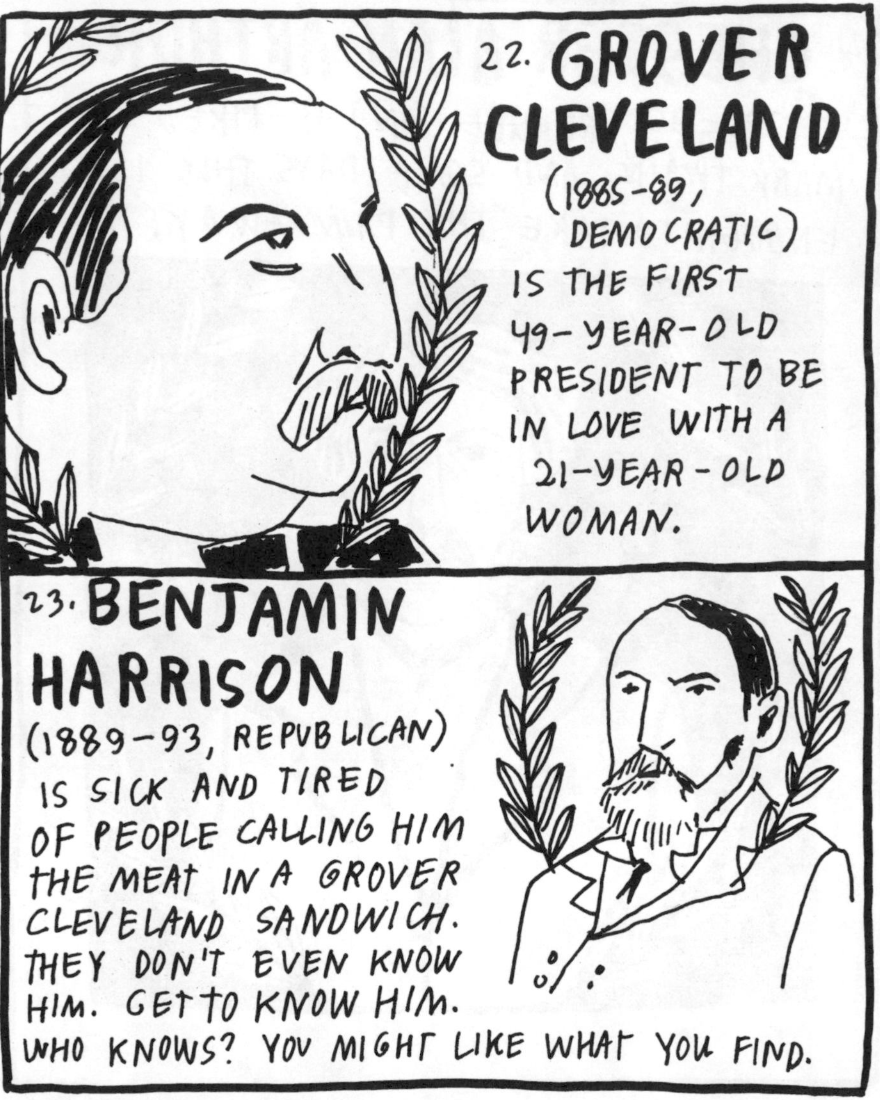
22. GROVER CLEVELAND
(1885-89, DEMOCRATIC)
IS THE FIRST 49-YEAR-OLD PRESIDENT TO BE IN LOVE WITH A 21-YEAR-OLD WOMAN.
23. BENJAMIN HARRISON
(1889-93, REPUBLICAN)
IS SICK AND TIRED OF PEOPLE CALLING HIM THE MEAT IN A GROVER CLEVELAND SANDWICH. THEY DON'T EVEN KNOW HIM. GET TO KNOW HIM. WHO KNOWS? YOU MIGHT LIKE WHAT YOU FIND.

24. GROVER CLEVELAND

(1893-97, DEMOCRATIC) THINKS MATH IS MATH, AND LOVE IS LOVE.

49 LESS 21 IS 28.

21 LESS 28 IS -7.

-7 GOES INTO 49 -7 TIMES.

-7 GOES INTO 21 -3 TIMES.

GROVER GOES INTO FRANCES.

NOW -3 AND -7 CAN'T GET EACH OTHER OUT OF EACH OTHER'S MINDS. FRANCES FOLSOM, WILL YOU MARRY GROVER CLEVELAND?

25. WILLIAM McKINLEY (1897–1901, REPUBLICAN)

IS CERTAIN THAT FUTURE MEDICAL TECHNO-LOGY WOULD HAVE RENDERED THIS INJURY NON-FATAL. HE RECKONS HE DESERVES IT, THOUGH, FOR INVADING THE PHILIPPINES AND CAMOUFLAGING IT AS <u>LIBERATION</u>. WILL THE FILIPINOS FORGIVE THE AMERICANS? THEY ALWAYS DO. WHAT DUPES!

26. THEODORE ROOSEVELT

(1901-09, REPUBLICAN) HAD A LOT OF FUN AT A PARTY OVER THE WEEKEND. IT WASN'T REALLY A PARTY, THOUGH. IT WAS MORE LIKE A WAR. HE STILL CAN'T BELIEVE THE FILIPINOS DECLARED WAR ON US! DESPITE THEIR FAULTS, THESE PEOPLE REALLY KNOW HOW TO HOST.

27. **WILLIAM HOWARD TAFT**

(1909-13, REPUBLICAN) IS SITTING IN HIS OVERSIZED TUB LETTING THE WATER RISE AND MAKE A ROSY BEIGE CONTINENT OF HIS BELLY. HE VISUALIZES HIMSELF ON THE BEACH ON HIS CONTINENT'S WESTERN SHORE RECLINING ON A STURDY, ERGONOMIC LOUNGE CHAIR UNDER AN UMBRELLA MADE OF BANANA LEAVES. FRANK SANTORO'S <u>STOREYVILLE</u> LIES OPEN ON HIS LAP TO PAGE 37, A GIANT PICTURE OF A SHIP SAILING AWAY INTO THE GENTLEST YELLOW LIGHT EVER SEEN. A YOUNG FILIPINO BOY STANDS BESIDE THE CHAIR ATTENDING TO GOVERNOR-GENERAL TAFT'S COMFORT. THE BOY RUNS BACK + FORTH FROM THE HOUSE BRINGING TAFT HALO-HALO, KALAMANSI JUICE, AND SARSI IN A BAG WITH A STRAW.

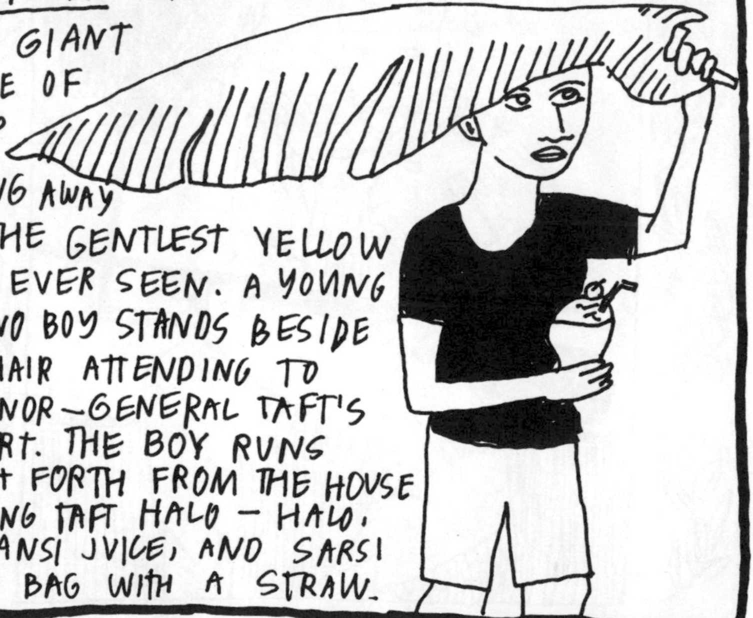

HE FANS TAFT'S FACE WITH A BANANA LEAF. "GOD DAMN," SAYS TAFT. "I MISS THIS PLACE."

28. WOODROW WILSON

(1913-21, DEMOCRATIC) HAS JUST RETURNED FROM AN APPOINTMENT WITH HIS DENTIST, WHO TOLD HIM THAT HE FOUND STRONG EVIDENCE THAT WILSON GRINDS HIS TEETH IN THE MIDDLE OF THE NIGHT.

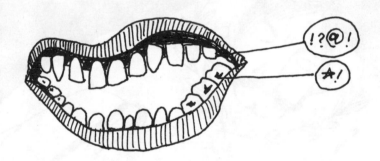

"THAT'S IMPOSSIBLE," WILSON REPLIED, "I'M ALWAYS UP IN THE MIDDLE OF THE NIGHT CHECKING MY GOOGLE."

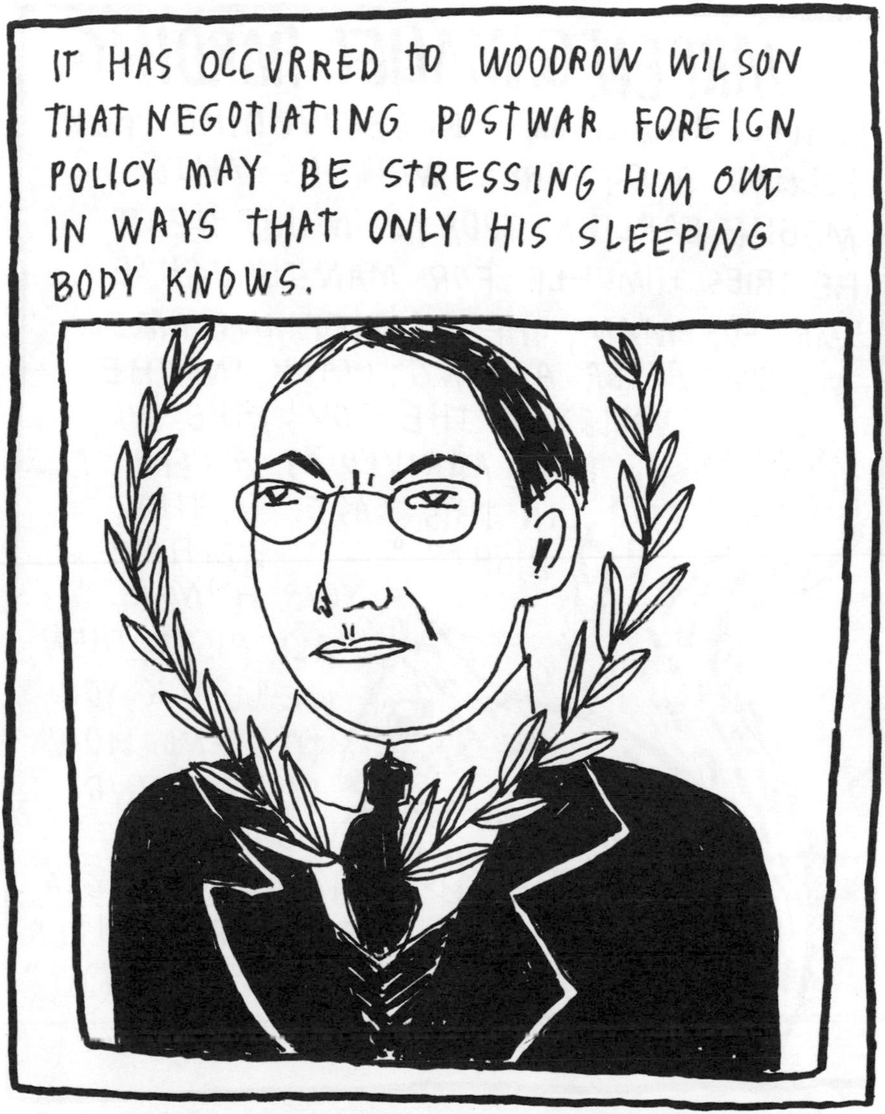
IT HAS OCCURRED TO WOODROW WILSON THAT NEGOTIATING POSTWAR FOREIGN POLICY MAY BE STRESSING HIM OUT IN WAYS THAT ONLY HIS SLEEPING BODY KNOWS.

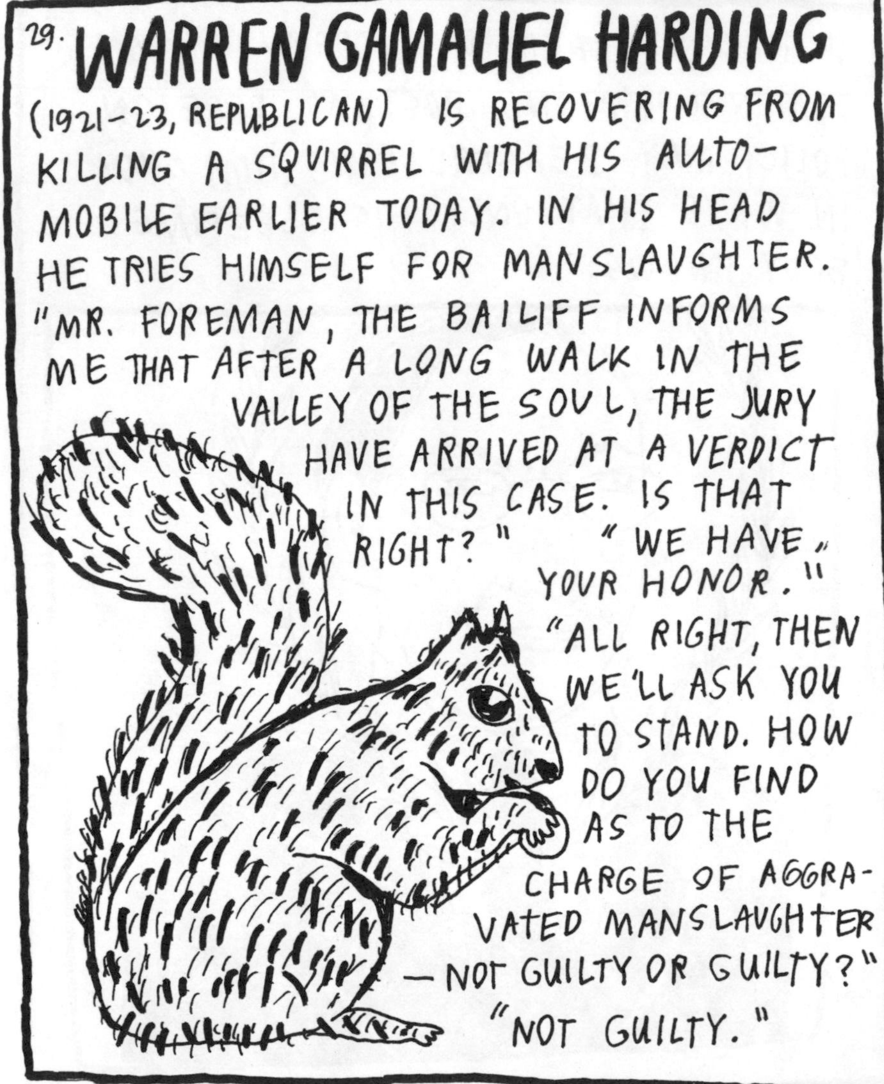
29. WARREN GAMALIEL HARDING
(1921-23, REPUBLICAN) IS RECOVERING FROM KILLING A SQUIRREL WITH HIS AUTOMOBILE EARLIER TODAY. IN HIS HEAD HE TRIES HIMSELF FOR MANSLAUGHTER. "MR. FOREMAN, THE BAILIFF INFORMS ME THAT AFTER A LONG WALK IN THE VALLEY OF THE SOUL, THE JURY HAVE ARRIVED AT A VERDICT IN THIS CASE. IS THAT RIGHT?" "WE HAVE, YOUR HONOR." "ALL RIGHT, THEN WE'LL ASK YOU TO STAND. HOW DO YOU FIND AS TO THE CHARGE OF AGGRAVATED MANSLAUGHTER —NOT GUILTY OR GUILTY?" "NOT GUILTY."

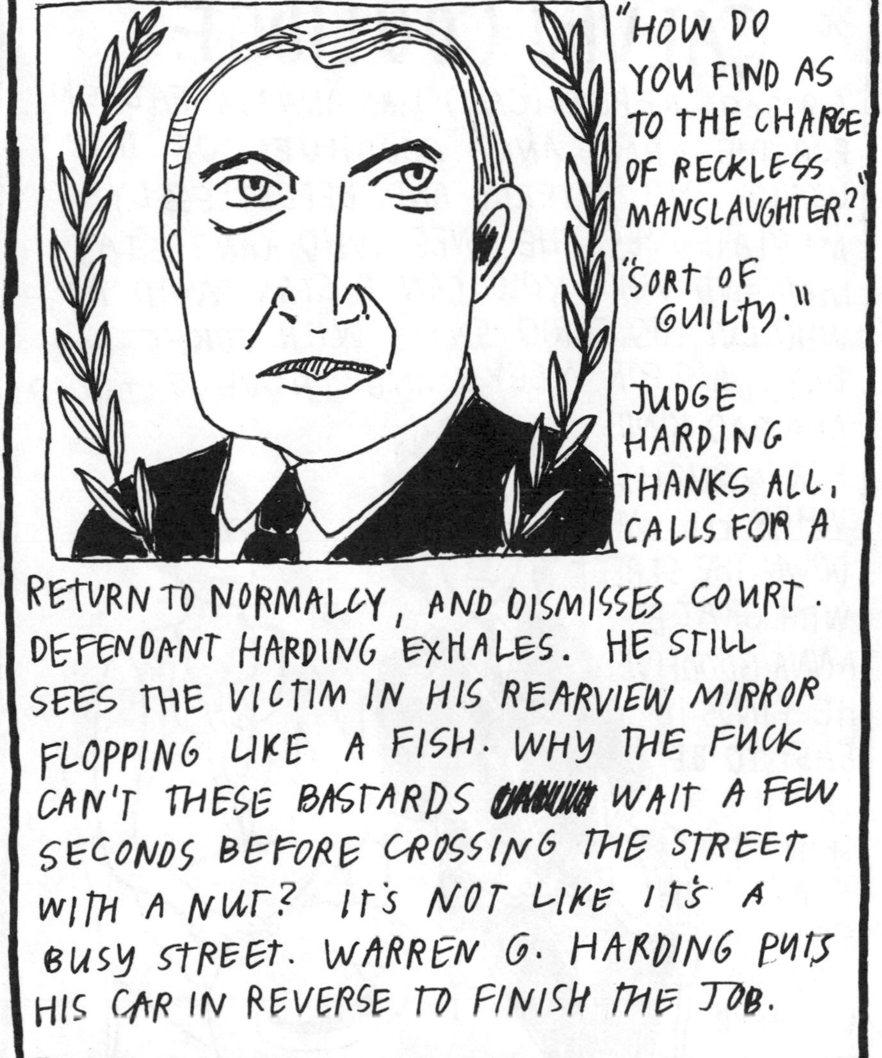
"HOW DO YOU FIND AS TO THE CHARGE OF RECKLESS MANSLAUGHTER?"
"SORT OF GUILTY."
JUDGE HARDING THANKS ALL, CALLS FOR A RETURN TO NORMALCY, AND DISMISSES COURT. DEFENDANT HARDING EXHALES. HE STILL SEES THE VICTIM IN HIS REARVIEW MIRROR FLOPPING LIKE A FISH. WHY THE FUCK CAN'T THESE BASTARDS WAIT A FEW SECONDS BEFORE CROSSING THE STREET WITH A NUT? IT'S NOT LIKE IT'S A BUSY STREET. WARREN G. HARDING PUTS HIS CAR IN REVERSE TO FINISH THE JOB.

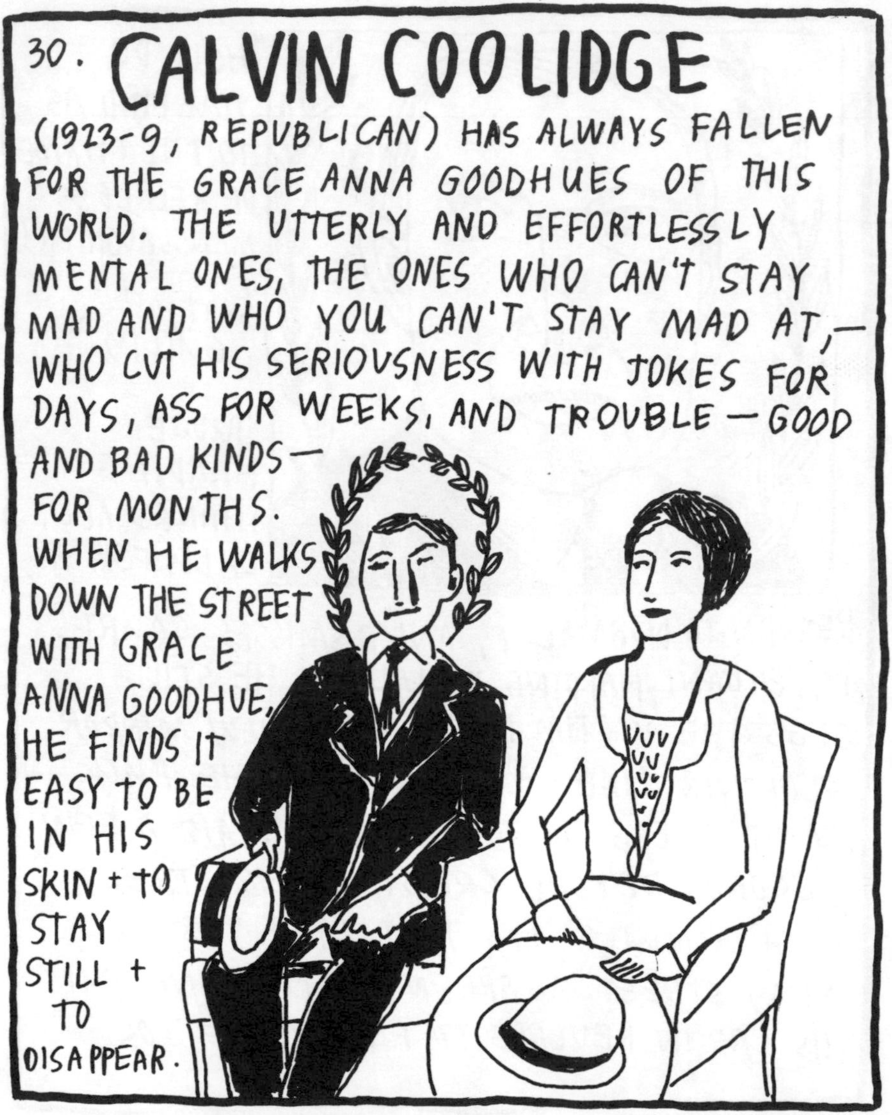
30. CALVIN COOLIDGE
(1923-9, REPUBLICAN) HAS ALWAYS FALLEN FOR THE GRACE ANNA GOODHUES OF THIS WORLD. THE UTTERLY AND EFFORTLESSLY MENTAL ONES, THE ONES WHO CAN'T STAY MAD AND WHO YOU CAN'T STAY MAD AT,— WHO CUT HIS SERIOUSNESS WITH JOKES FOR DAYS, ASS FOR WEEKS, AND TROUBLE—GOOD AND BAD KINDS— FOR MONTHS.
WHEN HE WALKS DOWN THE STREET WITH GRACE ANNA GOODHUE, HE FINDS IT EASY TO BE IN HIS SKIN + TO STAY STILL + TO DISAPPEAR.

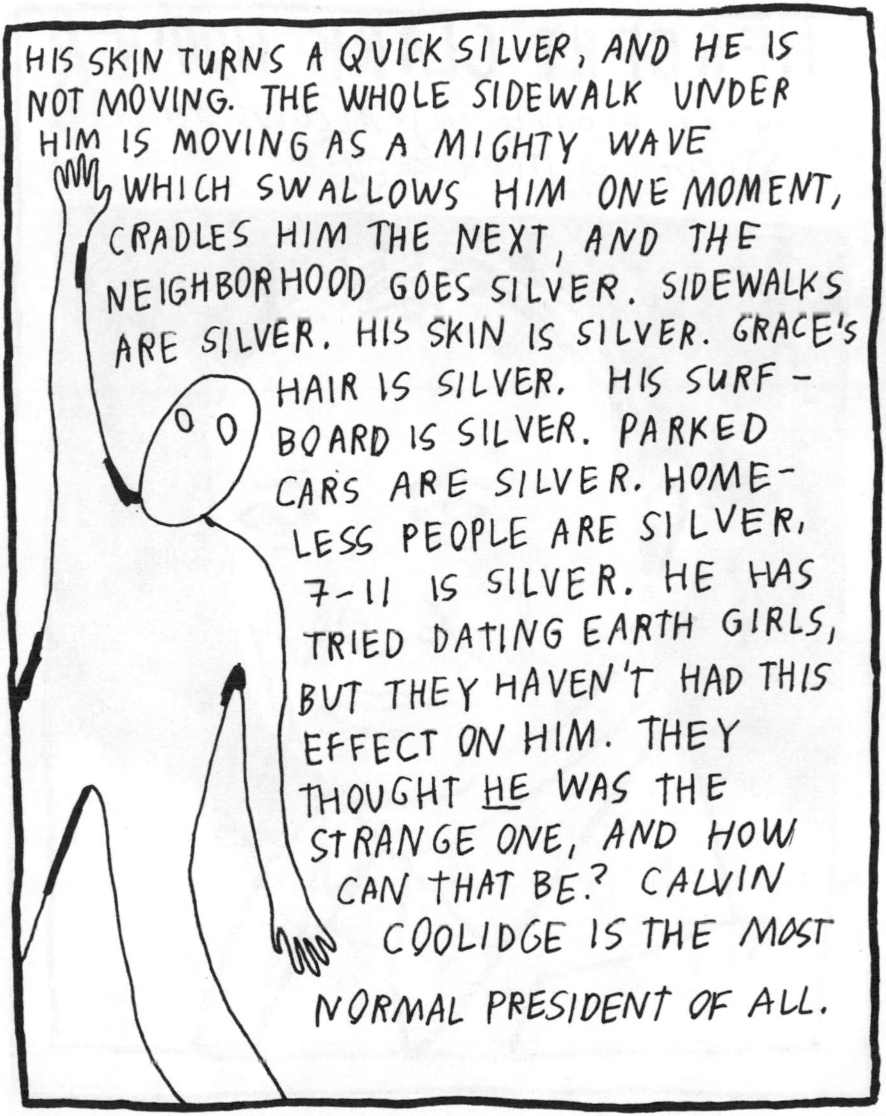
HIS SKIN TURNS A QUICK SILVER, AND HE IS NOT MOVING. THE WHOLE SIDEWALK UNDER HIM IS MOVING AS A MIGHTY WAVE WHICH SWALLOWS HIM ONE MOMENT, CRADLES HIM THE NEXT, AND THE NEIGHBORHOOD GOES SILVER. SIDEWALKS ARE SILVER. HIS SKIN IS SILVER. GRACE'S HAIR IS SILVER. HIS SURF-BOARD IS SILVER. PARKED CARS ARE SILVER. HOME-LESS PEOPLE ARE SILVER, 7-11 IS SILVER. HE HAS TRIED DATING EARTH GIRLS, BUT THEY HAVEN'T HAD THIS EFFECT ON HIM. THEY THOUGHT HE WAS THE STRANGE ONE, AND HOW CAN THAT BE? CALVIN COOLIDGE IS THE MOST NORMAL PRESIDENT OF ALL.

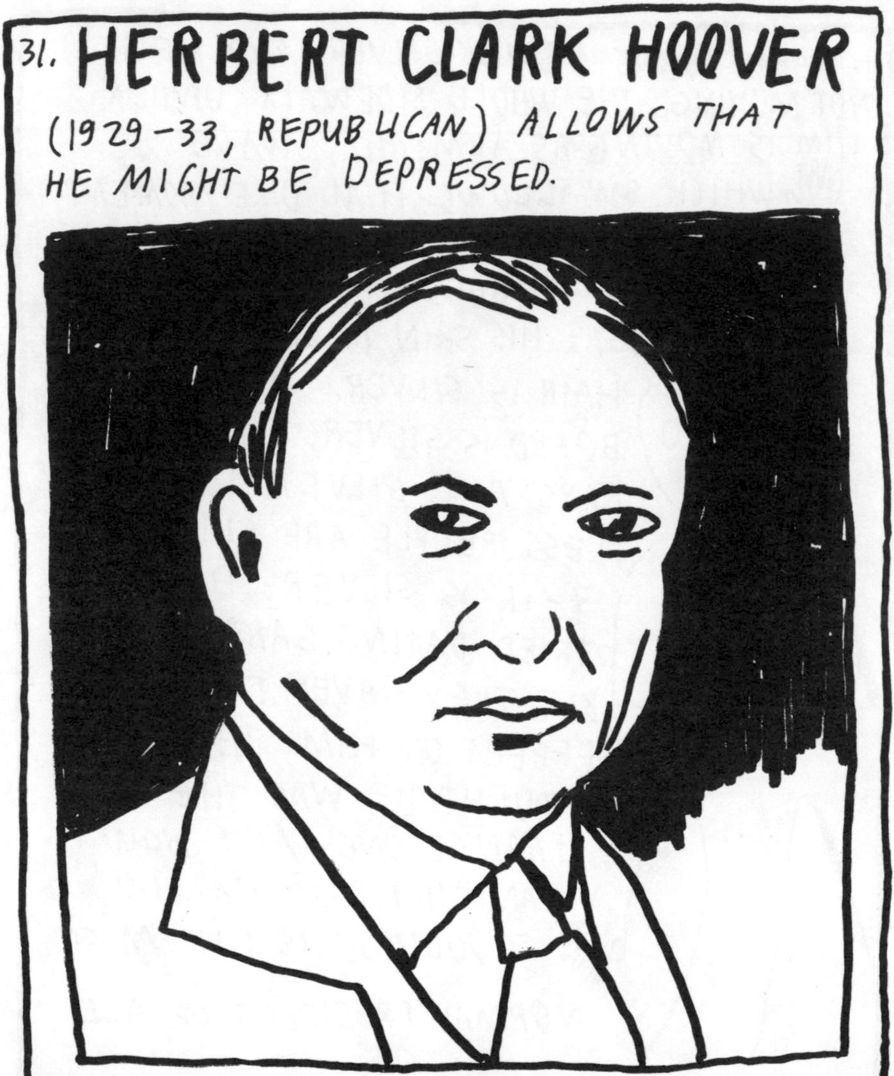
31. HERBERT CLARK HOOVER
(1929–33, REPUBLICAN) ALLOWS THAT HE MIGHT BE DEPRESSED.

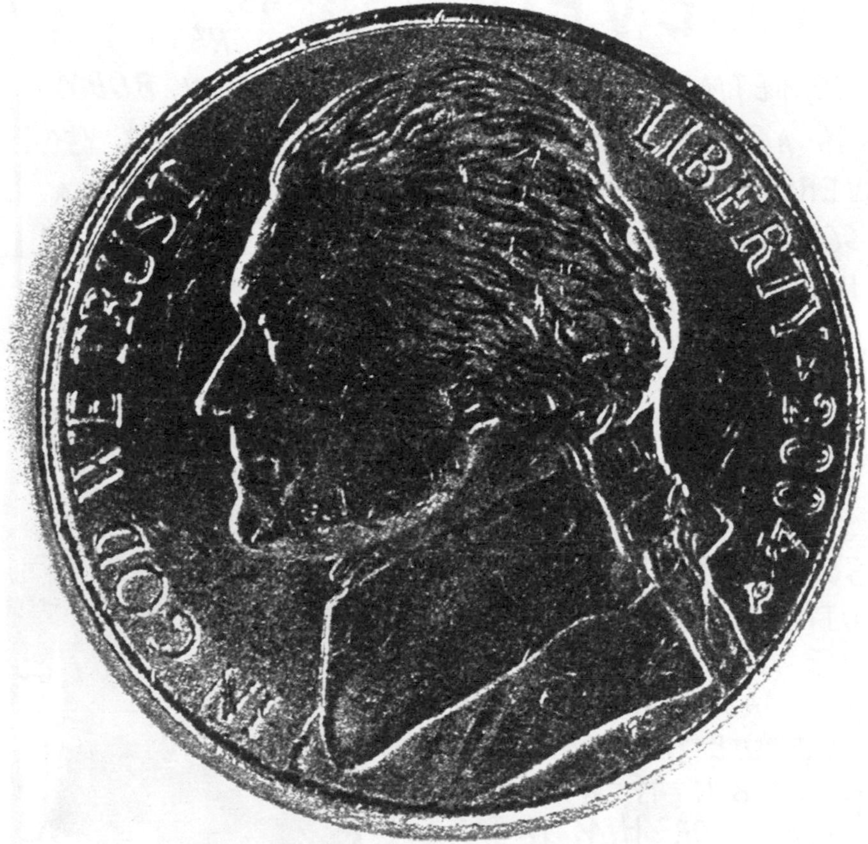
IN GOD WE TRUST
LIBERTY
2004

32. FRANKLIN DELANO ROOSEVELT (1933-45, DEMOCRATIC)

SOMETIMES FEELS AS IF HIS OWN BODY IS AGAINST HIM. HOWEVER, IT IS VERY, VERY, VERY IMPORTANT THAT NOBODY FEEL SORRY FOR HIM EVER. HE, FOR INSTANCE, HAS NEVER FELT SORRY FOR CHRIST. WHETHER OR NOT CHRIST IS A FAIRY TALE — LET'S BE REAL, HE'S SANTA CLAUS AND WILE E. COYOTE — NOT FEELING SORRY FOR HIM IS OF UTMOST IMPORTANCE. WE MAY ROOT FOR HIM; WE MAY WORRY ABOUT HIM; WE MAY MOCK HIM; BUT IF WE FEEL SORRY FOR HIM THEN HIS STORY IS USELESS.

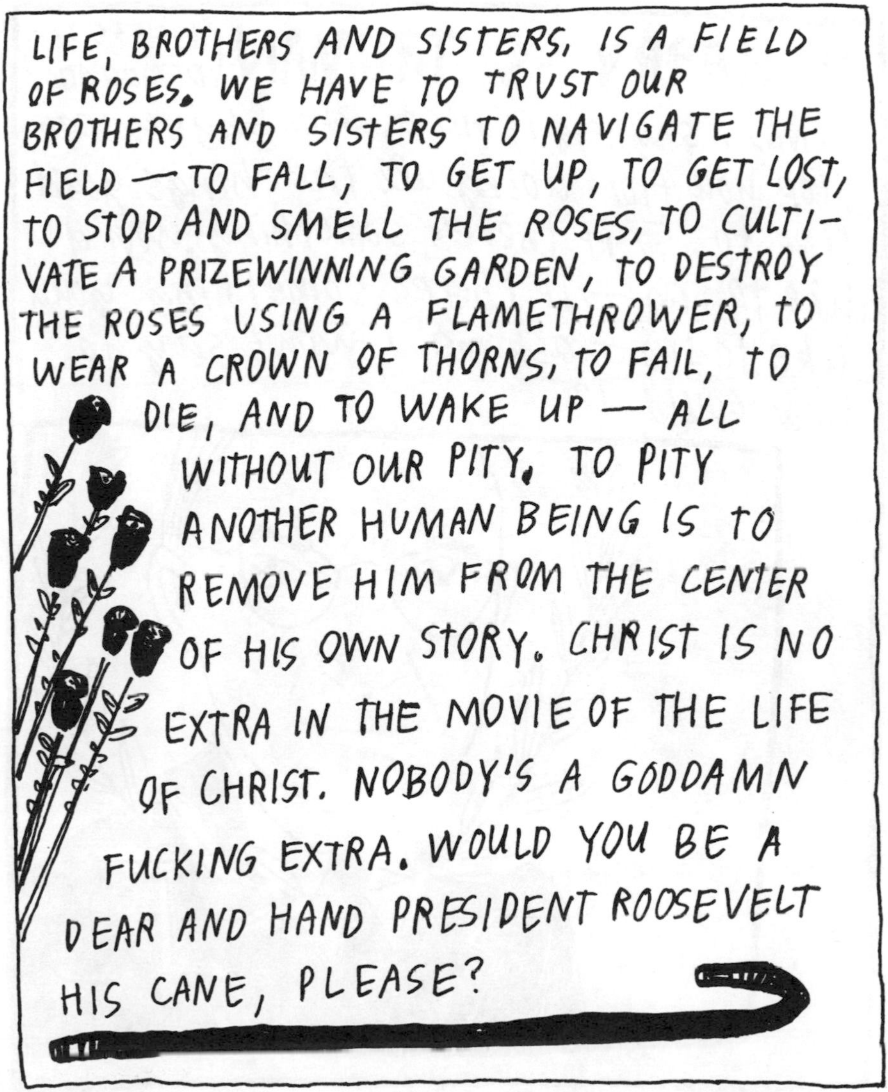
LIFE, BROTHERS AND SISTERS, IS A FIELD OF ROSES. WE HAVE TO TRUST OUR BROTHERS AND SISTERS TO NAVIGATE THE FIELD — TO FALL, TO GET UP, TO GET LOST, TO STOP AND SMELL THE ROSES, TO CULTIVATE A PRIZEWINNING GARDEN, TO DESTROY THE ROSES USING A FLAMETHROWER, TO WEAR A CROWN OF THORNS, TO FAIL, TO DIE, AND TO WAKE UP — ALL WITHOUT OUR PITY. TO PITY ANOTHER HUMAN BEING IS TO REMOVE HIM FROM THE CENTER OF HIS OWN STORY. CHRIST IS NO EXTRA IN THE MOVIE OF THE LIFE OF CHRIST. NOBODY'S A GODDAMN FUCKING EXTRA. WOULD YOU BE A DEAR AND HAND PRESIDENT ROOSEVELT HIS CANE, PLEASE?

33. HARRY S TRUMAN (1945-53, DEMOCRATIC)

SINGS, shyness is nice, and shyness can stop you from doing all the things you'd like to. So if there's something you'd like to try — if there's something you'd like to try — ask me, I won't say no, how could I?

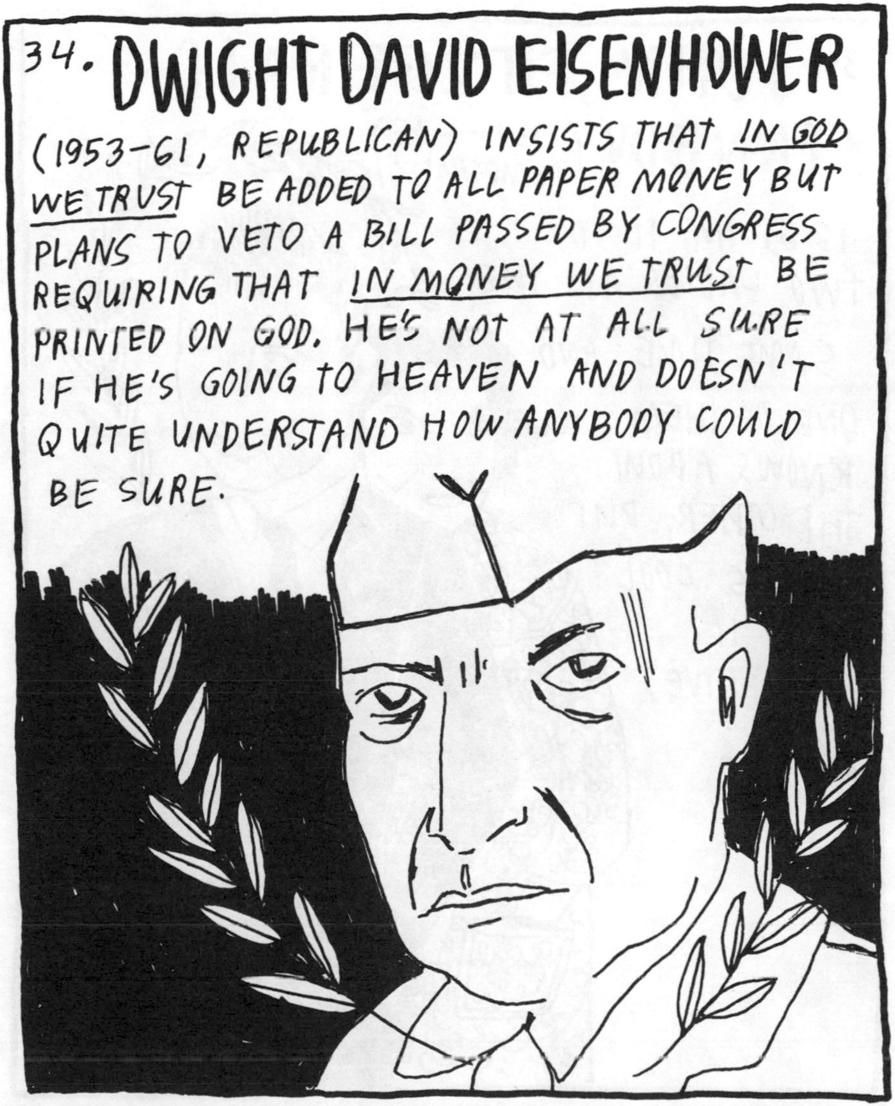
34. DWIGHT DAVID EISENHOWER
(1953-61, REPUBLICAN) INSISTS THAT IN GOD WE TRUST BE ADDED TO ALL PAPER MONEY BUT PLANS TO VETO A BILL PASSED BY CONGRESS REQUIRING THAT IN MONEY WE TRUST BE PRINTED ON GOD. HE'S NOT AT ALL SURE IF HE'S GOING TO HEAVEN AND DOESN'T QUITE UNDERSTAND HOW ANYBODY COULD BE SURE.

35. JOHN FITZGERALD KENNEDY (1961–63, DEMOCRATIC)

IS GIVING IT TO TWO LADIES AT THE SAME TIME, AND ONE OF THEM KNOWS ABOUT THE OTHER, BUT SHE IS COOL WITH IT. HIGH FIVE,

BRO.

36. LYNDON BAINES JOHNSON

(1963-69, DEMOCRATIC) IS POOR, GREW UP POOR, AND WILL ALWAYS BE POOR. YOU WOULDN'T UNDERSTAND IT, BUT POOR IS IN HIS BLOOD.

37. RICHARD MILHOUS NIXON

(1969-74, REPUBLICAN) VERY MUCH ENJOYED DARK KNIGHT AND DOESN'T CARE THAT ALL THE

OTHER PRESIDENTS DID TOO. HE LOVES THAT EVERY PRESIDENT HAS A DIFFERENT ANSWER WHEN YOU ASK "WHAT'S IT ALL ABOUT?" LBJ THINKS IT'S ALL ABOUT GAME THEORY. TEDDY'S IN IT FOR THE ACTION. LINCOLN FINDS THE SWEATY TENSION BETWEEN ITS PROTAGONIST AND ANTAGONIST INTERESTING, TO SAY THE LEAST. TRUMAN SAYS NOT LIKING DARK KNIGHT IS UNAMERICAN. DUBYA SWEARS IT'S HIM, HE'S BATMAN. AND NIXON, HE LIKES TO LISTEN IN ON THE OTHER GUYS. IT'S LIKE A MOVIE BEING PROJECTED ON ANOTHER MOVIE.

38. GERALD RUDOLPH FORD

(1974-77, REPUBLICAN) IS NOT SURE IF THE GIRL HE LIKES LIKES HIM BACK. I MEAN, YEAH, IT SEEMS LIKE MAYBE THEY ARE DATING JUST BY ACCIDENT. SHE NEVER VOTED HIM INTO OFFICE, AFTER ALL, BUT THAT'S OK. GERALD FORD IS OK WITH

BEING ALONE. HE CAN SEE BEING ALONE FOR THE REST OF HIS LIFE, BUT NEVER TO HAVE LOVE FOR SOMEBODY ELSE IS INCONCEIVABLE.

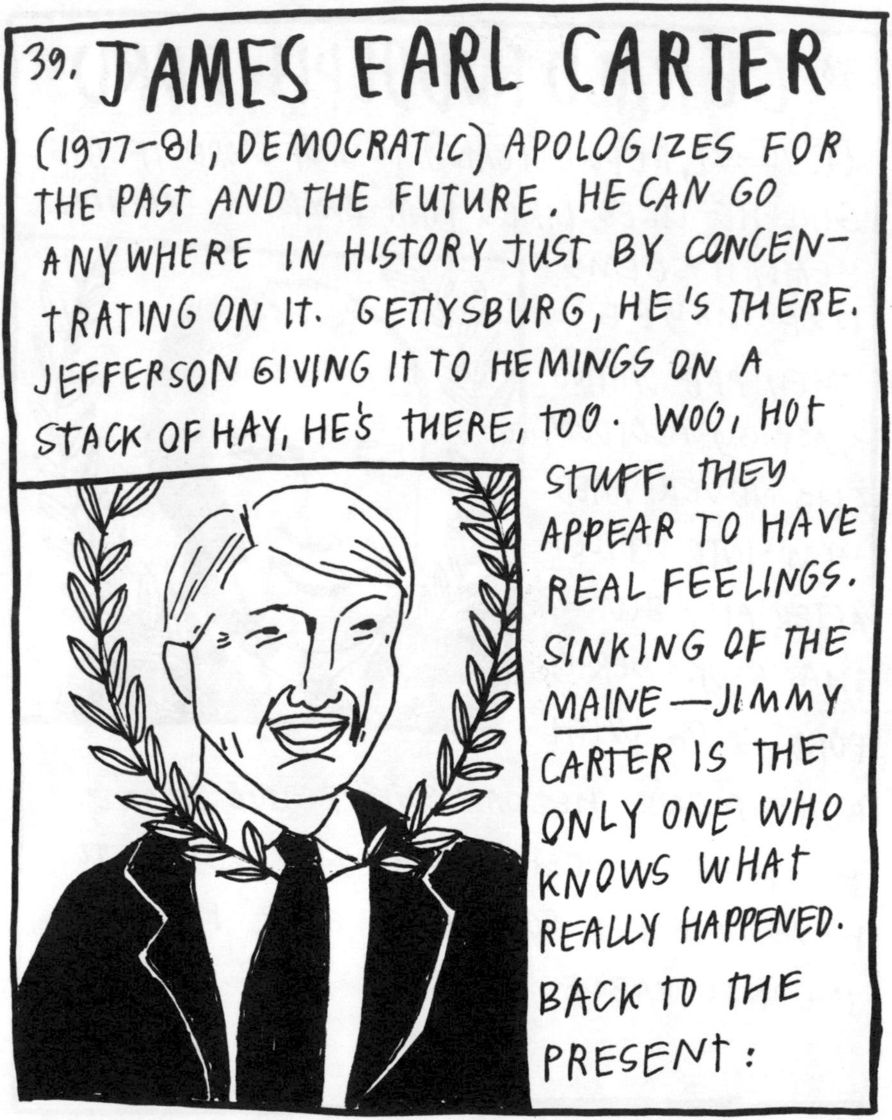
39. JAMES EARL CARTER
(1977–81, DEMOCRATIC) APOLOGIZES FOR THE PAST AND THE FUTURE. HE CAN GO ANYWHERE IN HISTORY JUST BY CONCENTRATING ON IT. GETTYSBURG, HE'S THERE. JEFFERSON GIVING IT TO HEMINGS ON A STACK OF HAY, HE'S THERE, TOO. WOO, HOT STUFF. THEY APPEAR TO HAVE REAL FEELINGS. SINKING OF THE MAINE—JIMMY CARTER IS THE ONLY ONE WHO KNOWS WHAT REALLY HAPPENED. BACK TO THE PRESENT:

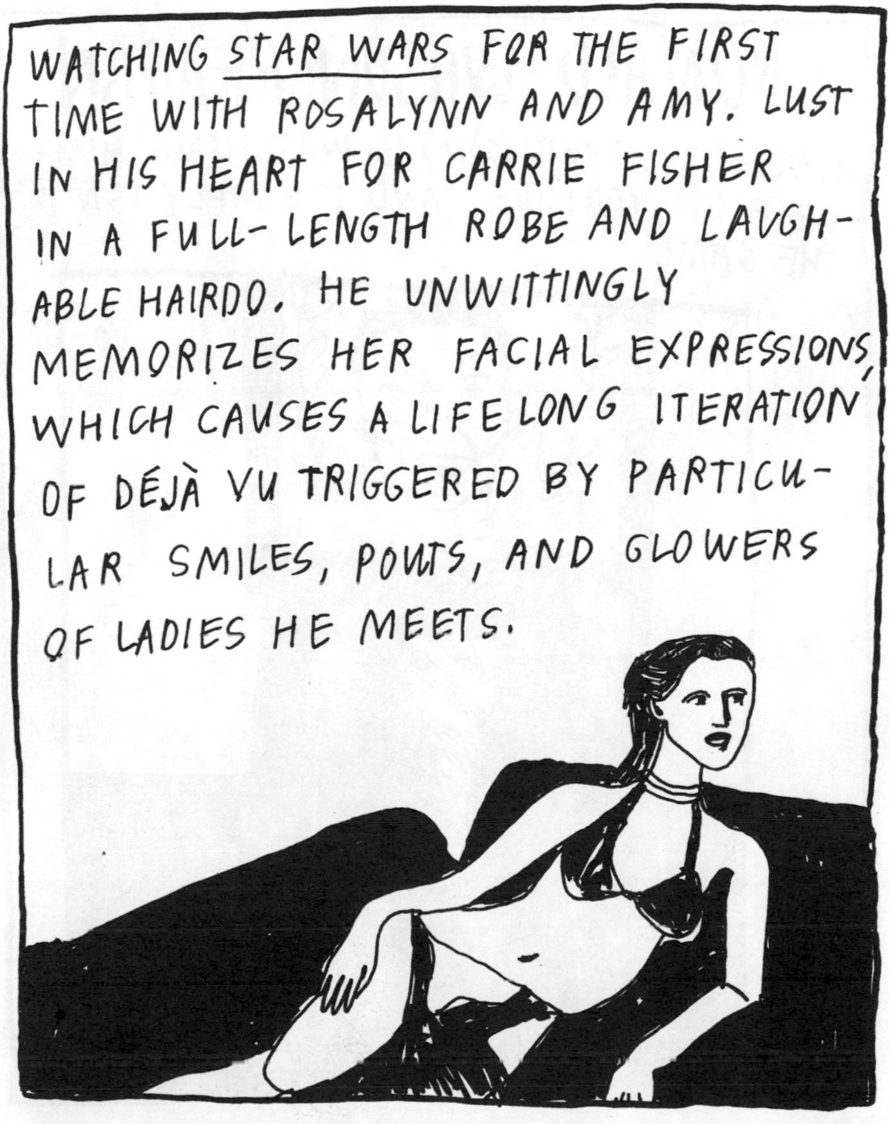
WATCHING STAR WARS FOR THE FIRST TIME WITH ROSALYNN AND AMY. LUST IN HIS HEART FOR CARRIE FISHER IN A FULL-LENGTH ROBE AND LAUGH-ABLE HAIRDO. HE UNWITTINGLY MEMORIZES HER FACIAL EXPRESSIONS, WHICH CAUSES A LIFELONG ITERATION OF DÉJÀ VU TRIGGERED BY PARTICU-LAR SMILES, POUTS, AND GLOWERS OF LADIES HE MEETS.

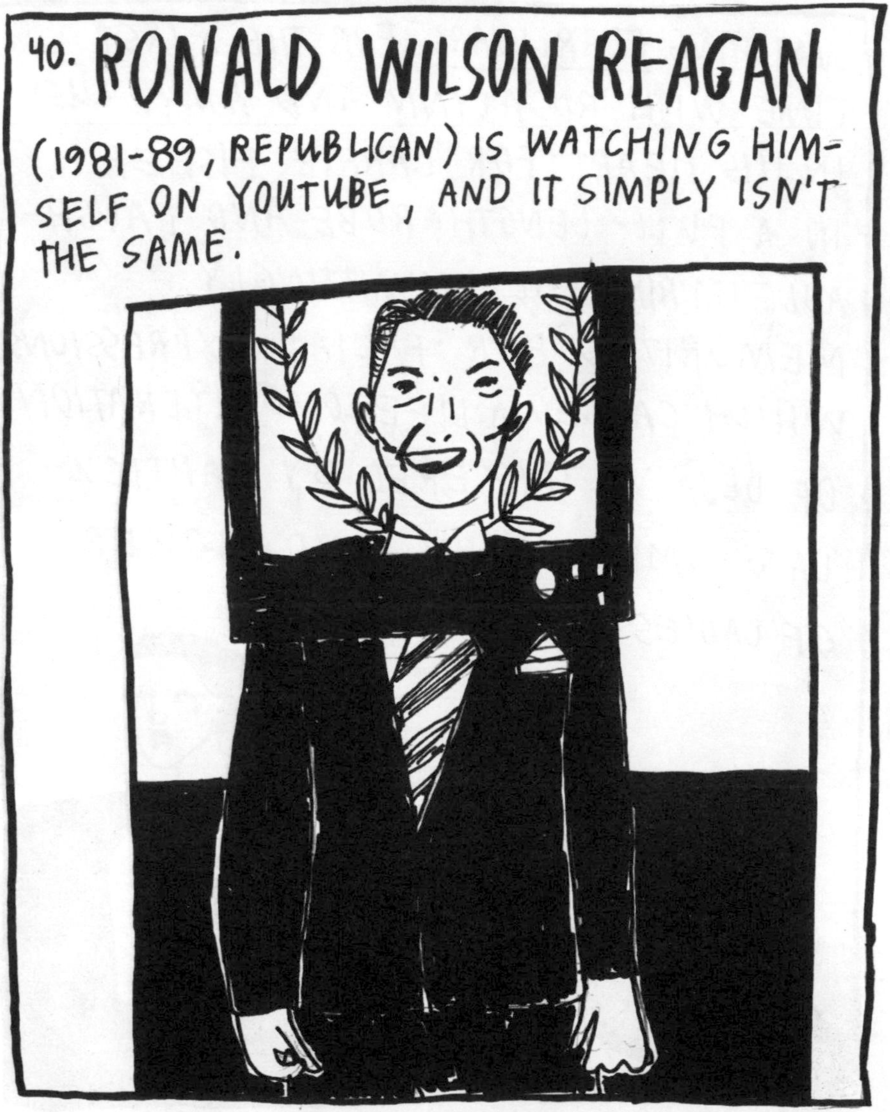
40. RONALD WILSON REAGAN
(1981-89, REPUBLICAN) IS WATCHING HIMSELF ON YOUTUBE, AND IT SIMPLY ISN'T THE SAME.

41. GEORGE HERBERT WALKER BUSH

(1989-93, REPUBLICAN) LOVES YOUTUBE, THOUGH.

HE LOVES TO WATCH A LOOP OF CLINTON SAYING HE DID NOT HAVE SEXUAL RELATIONS WITH THAT WOMAN, MONICA LEWINSKY, SET TO PET SHOP BOYS' "TO SPEAK IS A SIN." HE PRETENDS CLINTON IS PLAYING THE SAXOPHONE PART, AND LAUGHS. HOW DOES IT FEEL TO BE LAUGHING STOCK OF THE WORLD, GOLDEN BOY?

42. WILLIAM JEFFERSON CLINTON

(1993-2001, DEMOCRATIC) IS UPLOADING A HIGH-DEFINITION CLIP OF BUSH, SR. UPCHUCKING ON THE PRIME MINISTER OF JAPAN'S LAP.

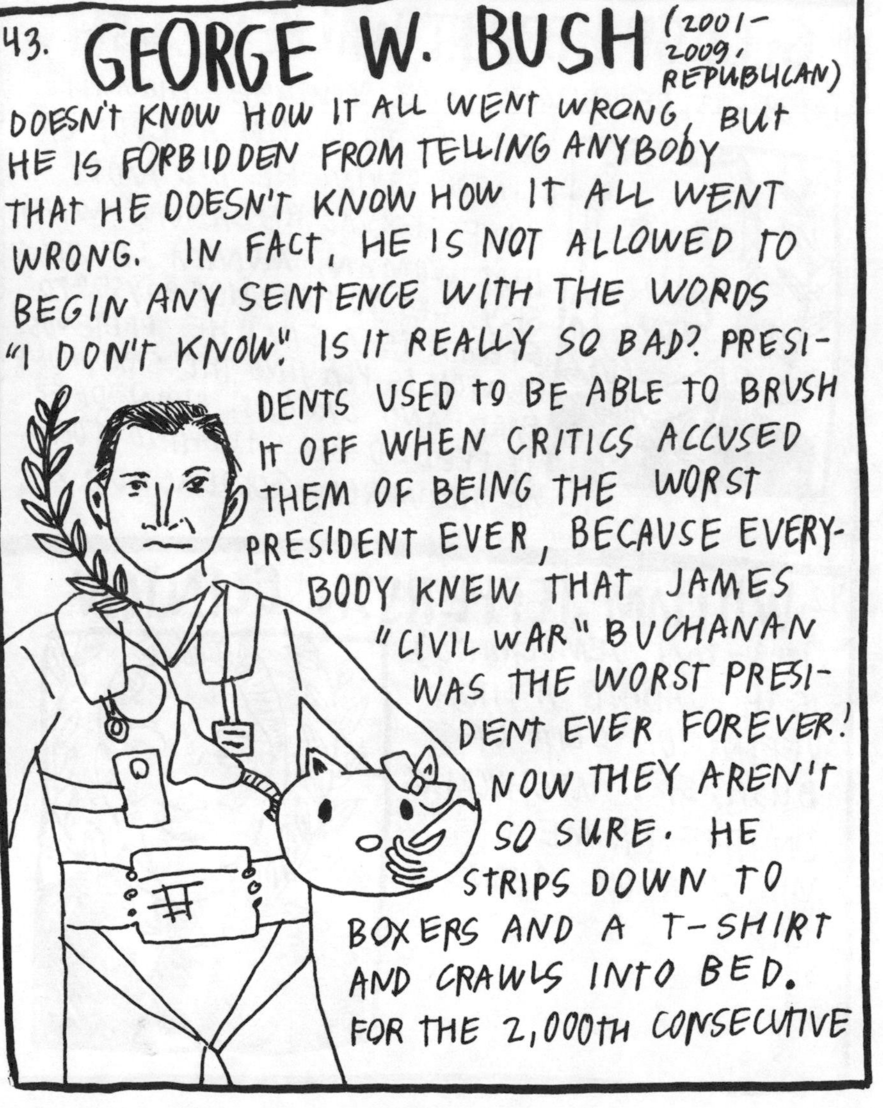
43. GEORGE W. BUSH (2001-2009, REPUBLICAN)
DOESN'T KNOW HOW IT ALL WENT WRONG, BUT HE IS FORBIDDEN FROM TELLING ANYBODY THAT HE DOESN'T KNOW HOW IT ALL WENT WRONG. IN FACT, HE IS NOT ALLOWED TO BEGIN ANY SENTENCE WITH THE WORDS "I DON'T KNOW." IS IT REALLY SO BAD? PRESIDENTS USED TO BE ABLE TO BRUSH IT OFF WHEN CRITICS ACCUSED THEM OF BEING THE WORST PRESIDENT EVER, BECAUSE EVERYBODY KNEW THAT JAMES "CIVIL WAR" BUCHANAN WAS THE WORST PRESIDENT EVER FOREVER! NOW THEY AREN'T SO SURE. HE STRIPS DOWN TO BOXERS AND A T-SHIRT AND CRAWLS INTO BED. FOR THE 2,000TH CONSECUTIVE

NIGHT, SLEEP WILL COME IN SPURTS.
HE'LL WAKE UP TO JOT DOWN SCRAPS OF
A DREAM IN HIS NOTEBOOK. TONIGHT
ALL THE TANKS, BOMBS, AND FIGHTER
PLANES HAVE A HELLO KITTY INSIGNIA
STENCILED ON THEIR SIDES, AND CON-
GRESS IS NOT ONE BIT PLEASED. WHAT'S
THEIR PROBLEM, IT'S NOT FUNNY? DUBYA
KNOWS THAT LIFE IS NOT FAIR AND
THAT HISTORY WILL NOT REMEMBER
HIM AS A FUN GUY, EVEN THOUGH
HE IS. A GENUINE GUY, A GUY WHO
HAS THOUGHT THINGS THROUGH. IT'S
TOO LATE, HE'S TOO OLD, NO ONE'S
AROUND. WELL THEN, HE WRITES, I'LL
JUST HAVE TO REMEMBER MYSELF
THAT WAY.

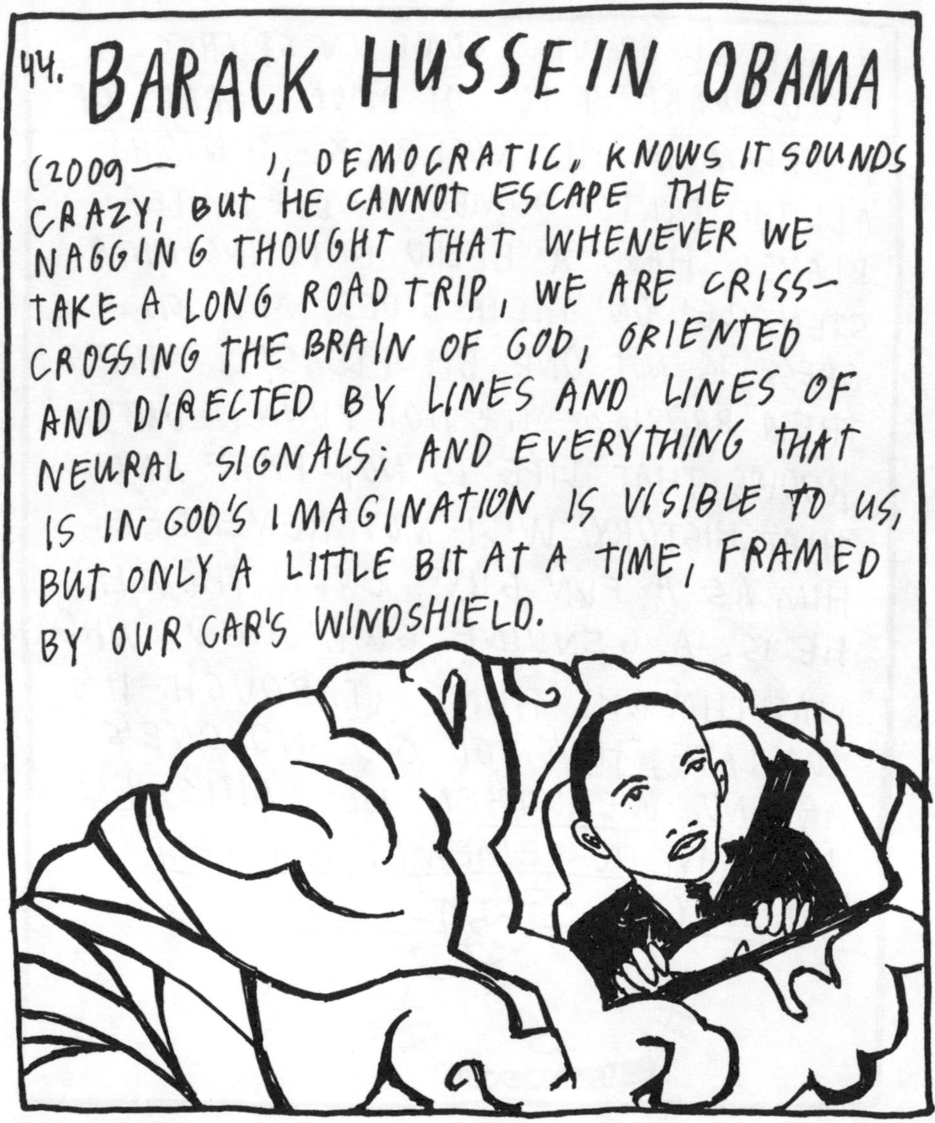
44. BARACK HUSSEIN OBAMA
(2009—), DEMOCRATIC, KNOWS IT SOUNDS CRAZY, BUT HE CANNOT ESCAPE THE NAGGING THOUGHT THAT WHENEVER WE TAKE A LONG ROAD TRIP, WE ARE CRISS-CROSSING THE BRAIN OF GOD, ORIENTED AND DIRECTED BY LINES AND LINES OF NEURAL SIGNALS; AND EVERYTHING THAT IS IN GOD'S IMAGINATION IS VISIBLE TO US, BUT ONLY A LITTLE BIT AT A TIME, FRAMED BY OUR CAR'S WINDSHIELD.

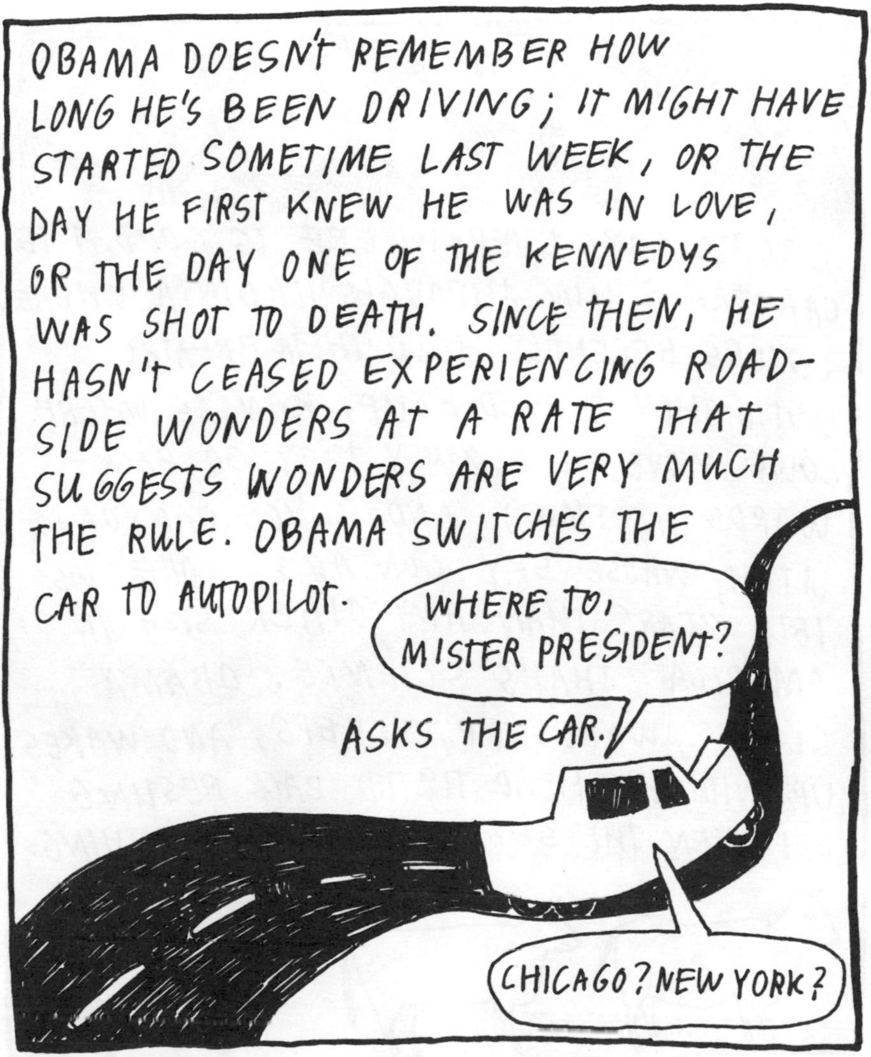
OBAMA DOESN'T REMEMBER HOW LONG HE'S BEEN DRIVING; IT MIGHT HAVE STARTED SOMETIME LAST WEEK, OR THE DAY HE FIRST KNEW HE WAS IN LOVE, OR THE DAY ONE OF THE KENNEDYS WAS SHOT TO DEATH. SINCE THEN, HE HASN'T CEASED EXPERIENCING ROAD-SIDE WONDERS AT A RATE THAT SUGGESTS WONDERS ARE VERY MUCH THE RULE. OBAMA SWITCHES THE CAR TO AUTOPILOT.
WHERE TO, MISTER PRESIDENT?
ASKS THE CAR.
CHICAGO? NEW YORK?

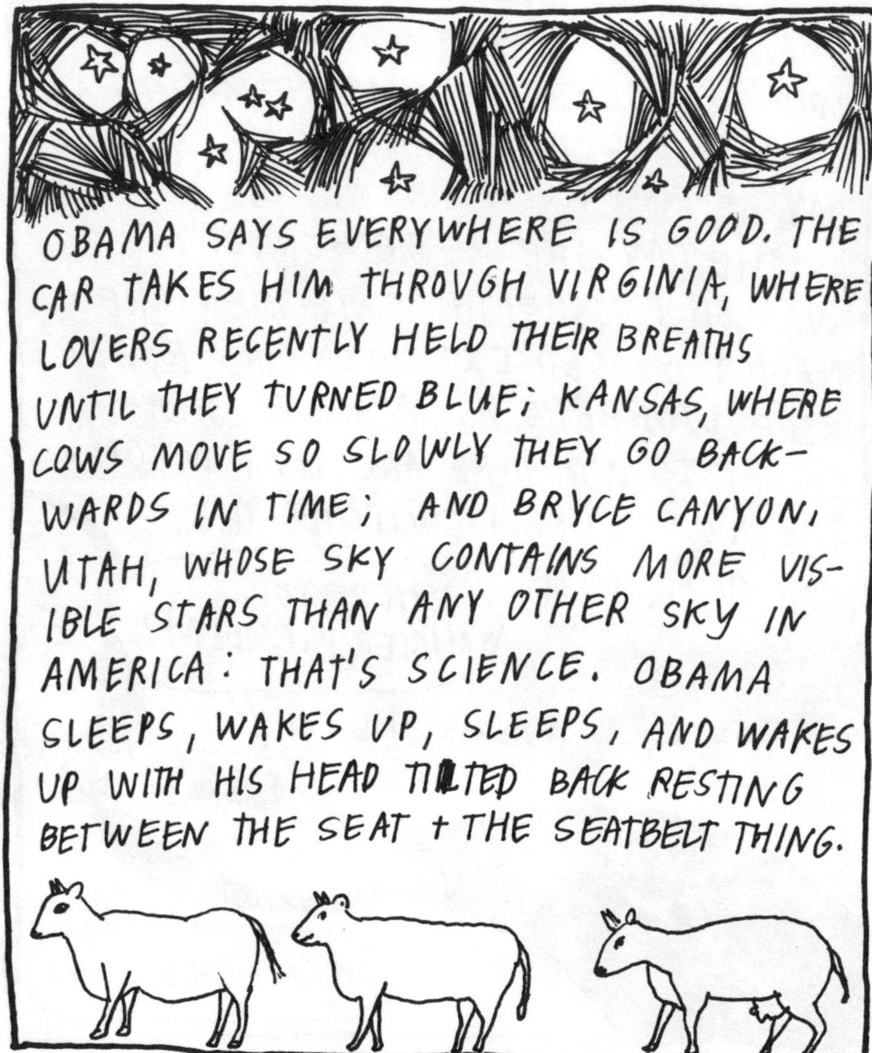
OBAMA SAYS EVERYWHERE IS GOOD. THE CAR TAKES HIM THROUGH VIRGINIA, WHERE LOVERS RECENTLY HELD THEIR BREATHS UNTIL THEY TURNED BLUE; KANSAS, WHERE COWS MOVE SO SLOWLY THEY GO BACK-WARDS IN TIME; AND BRYCE CANYON, UTAH, WHOSE SKY CONTAINS MORE VIS-IBLE STARS THAN ANY OTHER SKY IN AMERICA: THAT'S SCIENCE. OBAMA SLEEPS, WAKES UP, SLEEPS, AND WAKES UP WITH HIS HEAD TILTED BACK RESTING BETWEEN THE SEAT + THE SEATBELT THING.

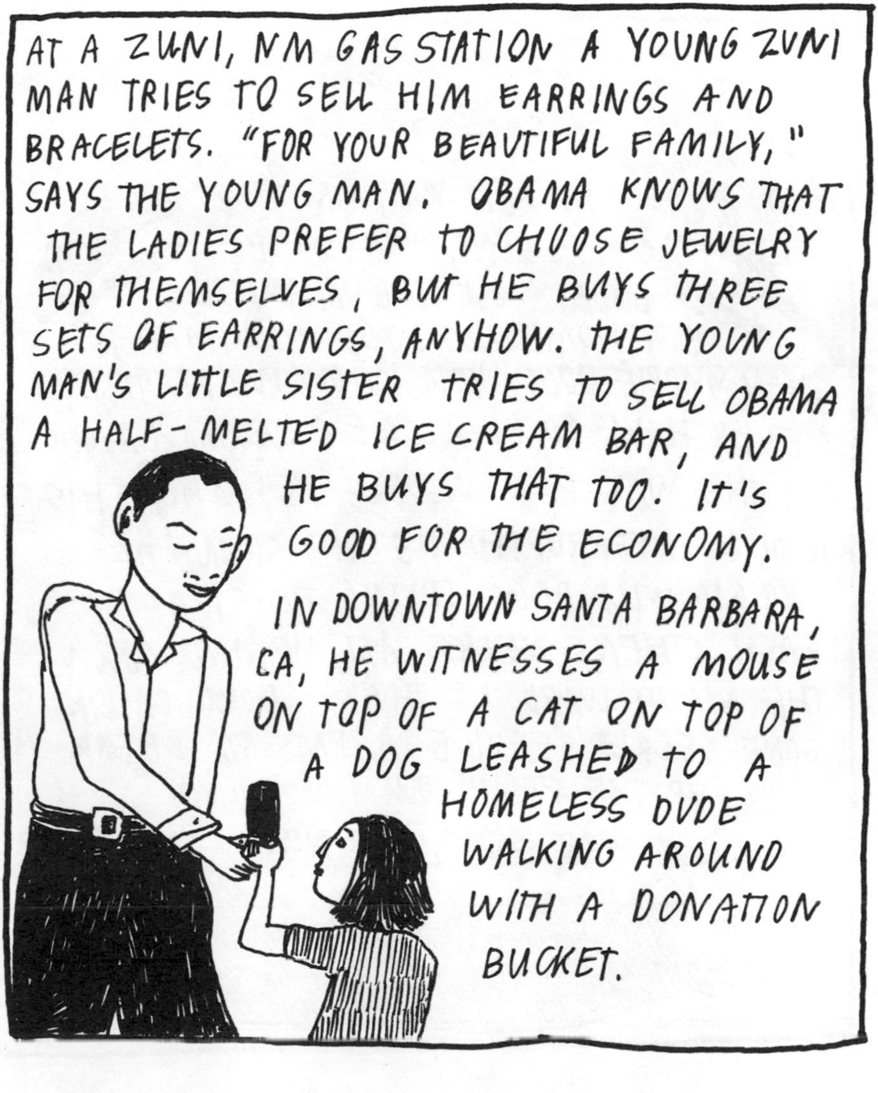
AT A ZUNI, NM GAS STATION A YOUNG ZUNI MAN TRIES TO SELL HIM EARRINGS AND BRACELETS. "FOR YOUR BEAUTIFUL FAMILY," SAYS THE YOUNG MAN. OBAMA KNOWS THAT THE LADIES PREFER TO CHOOSE JEWELRY FOR THEMSELVES, BUT HE BUYS THREE SETS OF EARRINGS, ANYHOW. THE YOUNG MAN'S LITTLE SISTER TRIES TO SELL OBAMA A HALF-MELTED ICE CREAM BAR, AND HE BUYS THAT TOO. IT'S GOOD FOR THE ECONOMY.
IN DOWNTOWN SANTA BARBARA, CA, HE WITNESSES A MOUSE ON TOP OF A CAT ON TOP OF A DOG LEASHED TO A HOMELESS DUDE WALKING AROUND WITH A DONATION BUCKET.

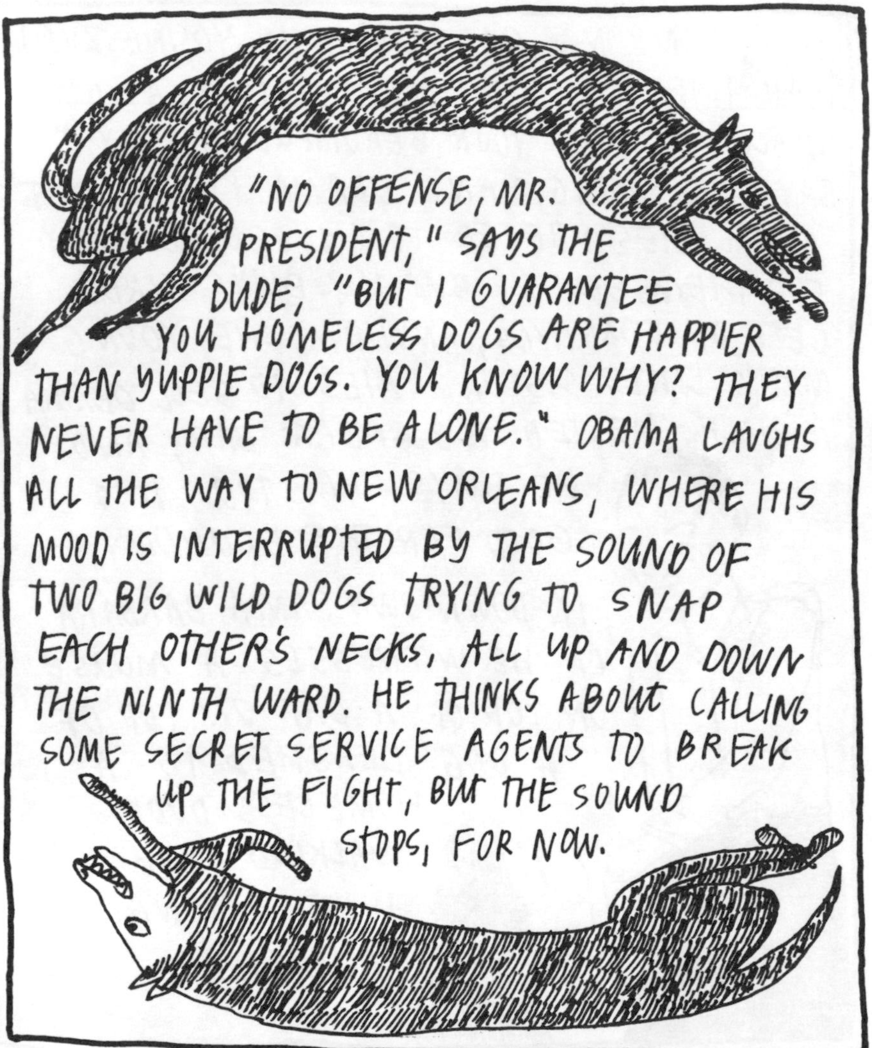
"NO OFFENSE, MR. PRESIDENT," SAYS THE DUDE, "BUT I GUARANTEE YOU HOMELESS DOGS ARE HAPPIER THAN YUPPIE DOGS. YOU KNOW WHY? THEY NEVER HAVE TO BE ALONE." OBAMA LAUGHS ALL THE WAY TO NEW ORLEANS, WHERE HIS MOOD IS INTERRUPTED BY THE SOUND OF TWO BIG WILD DOGS TRYING TO SNAP EACH OTHER'S NECKS, ALL UP AND DOWN THE NINTH WARD. HE THINKS ABOUT CALLING SOME SECRET SERVICE AGENTS TO BREAK UP THE FIGHT, BUT THE SOUND STOPS, FOR NOW.

ANYHOW, THERE ARE PROBABLY TWO BIG WILD DOGS FIGHTING ALL OVER THE COUNTRY, ALL OVER THE WORLD. IS HE SUPPOSED TO BE PRESIDENT TO ALL OF THEM? NOT A RHETORICAL QUESTION. HE CALLS UP HIS BEST FRIEND AND TELLS HER HIS IDEA FOR A NAME FOR THEIR NEW MUTT. SHE LAUGHS AND TELLS HIM SHE'LL RUN IT BY THE GIRLS.

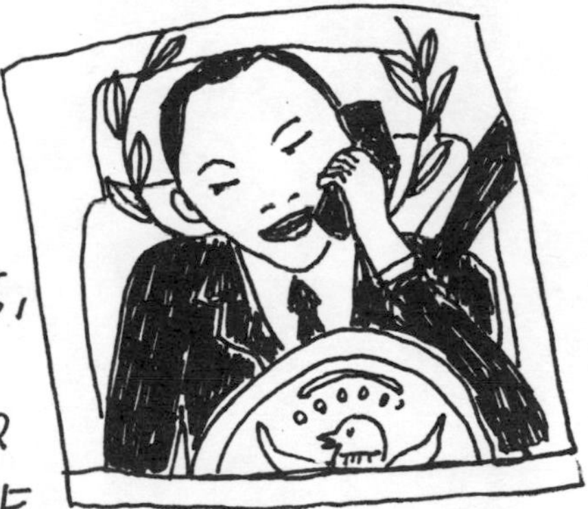

"I TAKE IT YOU WON'T BE HOME TONIGHT," SHE SAYS, WHICH CRACKS OBAMA UP. IT'S HER FAVORITE NEW JOKE, NOW THAT THE WHITE HOUSE IS A CAR.

ABOUT FORTY FOUR PRESIDENTS

FORTY FOUR PRESIDENTS ENVISIONS 220 YEARS OF PRESIDENTIAL SUCCESSION PANCAKED INTO A SINGLE MOMENT.

EACH COMMANDER-IN-CHIEF DOCUMENTS THE MOMENT THROUGH APHORISTIC "STATUS UPDATES" DESIGNED FOR EASY CONSUMPTION BY FACEBOOK FRIENDS. A JAUNTY, HIGH-CONTRAST PROFILE PICTURE REVEALS SOMETHING OF EACH PRESIDENT'S ESSENTIAL PERSONALITY (AND HOTNESS).

MZA WAS BORN TO FILIPINO IMMIGRANTS IN WASHINGTON, D.C. ON 16 MARCH 1973 AND HAS LOVED AMERICA EVER SINCE. HIS GRAND-FATHER MADE HIM POSSIBLE BY ESCAPING THE BATAAN DEATH MARCH IN 1942. HE LIVES IN VIRGINIA WITH A CAT.

MARIA SPUTNIK IS A REPORTER + A CARTOONIST.